What Others Are Saying A

INFLUENCED! is a rare book that not only inspires but also reorients you. Phil has captured something deeply true about life, leadership, and the quiet ways God shapes us over time. This isn't just another self-help book. It's a field guide for legacy.

Phil reminds us that we are all shaped by influence, visible, invisible, intentional, and accidental, and that gratitude isn't just a gentle virtue but a powerful transformational force. He writes with warmth, humility, and clarity that only comes through lived experience.

If you want to live your life with a deeper purpose, greater impact, and a renewed sense of calling, read this slowly. Reflect. Do the labs. This book will change how you see your past and how you invest in the future.

– **Dan Freschi**
President, EDGE – Where Leadership Begins
Author – *Where Leadership Begins*

INFLUENCED! deeply moved me. Phil's stories illuminate how influence quietly shapes a life, investing readers to pause, remember, and honor those who poured into them. It blends warmth, humility, and clarity, offering a gentle shift from self-made thinking to grateful stewardship. It is a beautifully reflective work that inspires intentional, legacy-minded living.

– **Jeremy Rush**
Executive Pastor – Spring Creek Church
Pewaukee, WI

My father used to tell me, "Son, it's a skinny piece of bread that only has one side." He meant that life and leadership always require openness to new perspectives, new solutions, and new people to invest in. Phil captures that same timeless truth in this work, INFLUENCED. Our greatest impact doesn't come from our earned titles alone; it comes from seeing there's another side to this bread and passing wisdom to others. This book is a masterclass in hidden influence, Legacy-Level Living, and the quiet ways God influences and grows people through us. It's the kind of book every leader needs, and my father would have loved.

– **Dan D'Amore**

Vice President, Sales & Marketing – AI Agents 4 Gov
President – Circuit Rider Ministries, Inc
Author – *Cybersecurity and AI for the Public Sector*

INFLUENCED!

INTRODUCTION

INFLUENCED!

Fulfillment **begins** with who shaped you
and **ends** with who's better
because of you

Phil Ransom

INFLUENCED!
Fulfillment begins with who shaped you and ends with who's better because of you
By: Phil Ransom
Published by: Vibrance Media

Author's Note:
Every day, you receive a 1440-minute auto-deposit of opportunity to live with gratitude, purpose, and influence. To help you stay intentional, download your free *1440 Tracker* and begin your legacy-level journey at **www.1440Tracker.com**

Disclaimer:
The information contained in this book is for general informational purposes only. The views expressed in this book are those of the author and do not necessarily reflect the views of the publisher. While the author has made every effort to ensure the accuracy and completeness of the information presented, the author and publisher assume no responsibility for errors, inaccuracies, omissions, or any other inconsistencies herein.

The advice and strategies contained herein may not be suitable for every situation. This book is sold with the understanding that the author and publisher are not engaged in rendering legal, accounting, medical, or other professional services. Readers should seek professional advice for their specific situation.

The author and publisher shall not be liable for any loss, damage, or injury, including but not limited to special, incidental, consequential, or other damages, caused or alleged to have been caused directly or indirectly by the information contained in this book.

Copyright © 2025, Phil Ransom, All Rights Reserved.

No part of this book may be reproduced in any form or by any electronic or mechanical means, including information storage and retrieval systems, without permission in writing from the publisher, except by a reviewer who may quote brief passages in a review.

If you find any typographical errors in this book, they're there for a reason. Some people love looking for them, and we strive to please as many people as possible.

Publishing Consultant: Erin Marie at www.ErinMarieBooks.com
ISBN: 979-8-9942996-0-9
First Edition, 2025
Printed in the United States of America
10 9 8 7 6 5 4 3 2 1

Dedication

~ Brenda ~
You've lived much of this work before it came to be.
Devoted, steady, pray-first faith
through each season that came.
Generous cups of cold water
from your deep well of love for God and our family.
Resilience that meets each day with grace,
despite MS's attempts to sabotage your joy.
To you I dedicate this, my first book.
Phil

Contents

Forward		i
Introduction		1
Chapter 1	You've Been Influenced	9
Chapter 2	Hidden Mentors	35
Chapter 3	Arrival vs. Legacy	51
Chapter 4	Gratitude: The Transformation Engine	71
Chapter 5	Return on Invested Influence	119
Chapter 6	The Power of Strategic Advocacy	139
Conclusion	A Note From Me in Your Desk Drawer	143

FOREWORD
by Dan Freschi

I have always believed that leadership begins inside a person long before it ever shows up on the outside. Before decisions, before direction, and before influence, there is a forming, a shaping of who we are and what we value.

But as I've grown older, and hopefully a little wiser, I've realized something else:

What is formed inside us didn't start with us.

When Phil first shared the heart behind *INFLUENCED!*, I felt something stir that was familiar and deeply personal. Because this book isn't just about leadership or influence, it's about all the people, named and unnamed, who poured something into us, who believed in us at moments we didn't even believe in ourselves, who nudged us into becoming what we couldn't yet see.

If I'm honest, I don't know where I'd be without those people in my life *(Mrs. Baldwin, Guy Worth, the Lopezs, the Yamaguchis, Maj. Desjardin, LTC Wines, LTC McCombs, Dan Gaynor, Phil Lacorte, and Dominic and Joann Freschi, to mention a few).* People who saw potential I didn't recognize, who cracked doors open when I didn't know a door existed, and who spoke words that still echo in my mind today. Some of them did this intentionally while others influenced me without realizing the impact they were having.

When I read Phil's stories, his music teacher, his aunt, the professor who pulled a hidden gift to the surface, it took me back to my own moments. The ones that shape you quietly and permanently. The ones you carry with you for decades, sometimes without even realizing it.

And that's what makes this book so meaningful. Phil crafts words to express feelings most of us have experienced but never put into words. He provides language for the gratitude we carry but often struggle to articulate. He shows us that influence isn't just a leadership tactic. It's an essential part of who we are.

This book feels like taking a walk through the hallways of your own life, pausing at faces you haven't thought about in years, remembering conversations that mattered more than you realized at the time. And then somewhere along the way, you start understanding something profound:

If others shaped us this much, then we have the privilege and responsibility to shape others, too.

That shift from reflection to stewardship is what makes *INFLUENCED!* More than just a book. It's an invitation. A gentle, personal, and gracious invitation to live intentionally and focus less on accumulating achievements, and more on leaving a trail of people who are better for having encountered you.

Phil writes with such humility, such honesty, and such generosity of spirit that you can't help but feel encouraged. He doesn't posture. He doesn't preach. He opens up his life and lets you see the fingerprints of God and others all over it. This reflects how God works through His people.

If you're anything like me, you'll finish this book with a renewed appreciation for the people who God put in front of you, who chose to invest in you, and with a newfound desire to be that kind of person for someone else.

So, take your time. Sit with the stories. Let the gratitude rise.

And as you do, I hope you'll see what I've seen:

None of us became who we are alone. And none of us has to settle for letting our influence end with us.

Phil has written something beautiful, honest, and needed.

And I'm grateful to be able to say:

This isn't just a book worth reading. It's a book worth living.

Godspeed.

Dan Freschi
President, EDGE – Where Leadership Begins
Author – *Where Leadership Begins*

INTRODUCTION

Defining moments like to work solo. We seldom notice when one is approaching. Quietly and unannounced, a defining moment will slip silently into life's theater, take a seat next to you without a word,
and wait.

Then— at just the right moment, it'll lean briefly into your shoulder. You'll notice and glance over to see it point to the life-size screen, and whisper, " *You'll never forget this. Look."*

Three of my defining moments, each about a decade apart, have profoundly affected my life and work.

My wife and I traveled to the Utah Rockies for my Grandpa Ransom's memorial service in May 1980. He'd been diagnosed with Stage 4 brain cancer in November and passed away peacefully at home 5½ months later. After the funeral, while many of the family visited, two of my cousins and I mustered up the courage to ask Grandma if we could go for a drive in Grandpa's car. She agreed and motioned to Vic, the oldest, where he'd find the keys. Vic, Steve, and I meandered around town, playing memory tapes of our growing-up years, remembering, laughing, recalling the places Grandpa and Grandma had lived and the lives they touched, including ours. I, the youngest of the three, had the back seat to myself.

Here's the moment when life pointed and whispered, "Look."

Turn today's 1440 minutes into momentum.
Download your free tracker at 1440Tracker.com

Pulling away from a stop sign, Vic sighed.

"Grandpa was barely 5'4". Why do I feel so small?"

Good question. We talked about it for a few minutes and decided maybe it was because he and Grandma poured themselves into the people they served. So far as we could remember, they always had. Grandpa read & studied voraciously, was an excellent pastor and teacher who loved spending time with family, fishing, pheasant hunting, playing Scrabble and other games. Many people had benefited from his life and work over the years. Less than a year before his diagnosis, Grandpa and my dad were on my ordination council, and both spoke at the ordination service. Dad was much like Grandpa, and I looked up to them. In my mid-20s, enjoying early success in my ministry, I silently resolved to carry on their legacy.

-=-=-=-

While enjoying lunch with a group of fellow grad students in Chicago, ten years later, Bill Hull, one of our Moody Graduate School professors, looked in my direction. "Phil, I have a question for you. I've read your pre-course work, you're participating in class, and I'm wondering. You're gifted in the areas of teaching and administration, is that correct?" I nodded. "There are several styles or models for teaching and administering, and you've chosen one. Why did you choose your style, do you know?" (I didn't.) He asked a couple more questions, maybe to confirm in his mind that what he was about to say was accurate, then took a deep breath.

(Here's the whispered "Look. There's more here than you're seeing.")

Turn today's 1440 minutes into momentum.
Download your free tracker at 1440Tracker.com

"I'd like to suggest, if I may, that you have one more gift. Encouragement, and *it's* the one that drives your teaching and administration." I thanked him for his keen insight.

I returned home from that week on campus with a more profound sense of purpose that, from that day forward, affected how I treat the volunteers I work with, the lessons & talks I prepare, and the programs I create.

-=-=-=-

I made sure I included a visit with my Aunt Pauline on my 2001 ministry trip to observe and interview worship arts leaders in churches led by strong pulpiteers. My mom's younger sister, Pauline, lived in Seabrook, Texas, on Galveston Bay. Her delightful home rose above the surf on stilts, should a hurricane or tropical storm come her way. The salty air somehow felt medicinal. As a kid, I'd always wished I could hang out with the adults at family gatherings and enjoy their conversations. Aunt Pauline's gentle Texas accent captivated my kid from the high plains attention. But— I was one of the cousins, so I heard "go play" more often than I cared to. While visiting her, she showed me several local sites.

We meandered our way through long conversations, and she treated me to the freshest seafood I'd ever tasted at a little place on the bay. A respected English teacher, Aunt Pauline had agreed to read and review my master's thesis (I still have her notes), and I sought her perspective on several aspects of what I'd written.

At one point, Aunt Pauline stated with gentle confidence, "I believe you have a book in you, Phil. At least one, maybe more."

Turn today's 1440 minutes into momentum.
Download your free tracker at 1440Tracker.com

"Seriously?" I made sure I heard her correctly.

"Yes," she smiled, her low alto voice confirming, "I believe you do."

It's taken much too long, but you're holding that book.

-=-=-=-

Each of those moments arrived while I was doing good work and making progress. Each of those moments pointed to life's big screen, *"Look. There's more."*
Each urged me on and called me higher.
Each was an unexpected realization, a defining moment.

Looking back on these and countless other realizations, I've come to hold that having a positive influence on people is the best legacy one can leave. I invite you to join me in living a life of the utmost meaning.

Look. There's more.

Your Invitation to Legacy-Level Living

About halfway through his book, Halftime (©1994), author Bob Buford wrote:

> "As we move closer to the halftime of our lives, we realize that we can only buy, sell, manage and attain so much. We also begin to understand that we will only *live* so long. When all is said and done, our success will be pretty empty
>
> unless it has included a corresponding degree of significance—and much of what we do in the first half is not imbued with the presence of the eternal." (p. 108)

Turn today's 1440 minutes into momentum.
Download your free tracker at 1440Tracker.com

May I share a little secret with you?
You don't have to wait that long to notice. That you're reading this tells me you're at least entertaining the possibility that there's more than what culture's serving in its buffet.

Most dictionaries include at least one definition of success that mentions "it isn't countable". King Solomon had more countable wealth than anyone before him, but his assessment of wealth was less than optimistic. (You can find his words in the book of Ecclesiastes if you need something depressing to read.)

There's more to a great legacy than houses, lands and investment accounts to divvy up between the kids & grandkids, and major gifts to favorite charities. Legacy-Level Living involves people. Hope. Vision. And love, or at least like. Because Legacy-Level Living is subjective, the generous don't bother to count or keep score. They invest freely, knowing they'll learn how things turned out sometime later, if at all.

Soon after my defining moment high in the Rockies, talking with my cousins in the car Grandpa no longer needed, I wrote:

Everything I know, I have learned from someone.
It's my responsibility to add to it before passing it along.

I'm grateful all those people trusted me with what they knew. I'm going to steward their investment in me wisely and add reliable information & wisdom to it, so it remains valuable to the next in line.

Legacy-Level Living is rooted in gratitude. It includes conscientious care. And it requires generosity.

Legacy-Level Living influence uses a different playbook:

- ✓ There's less striving and more stewarding;
- ✓ It recognizes what we've received and is grateful, then it shares. Duplicates. Invests in another.
- ✓ It reframes how we view our current capacity rather than adding another burden. I think you'll love that.

We'll unwrap this concept in INFLUENCED. I invite you to honestly consider the benefits of living this way. I hope you agree that it isn't something more to do; it's a liberating—and the most rewarding—way to live.

What This Book Will Do & How to Read it

INFLUENCED has 3 parts:
Recognition, Transformation, & Application

Part 1 will help you identify who has influenced you, understand how influence works, and acknowledge some of your hidden contributors.

Part 2 will help you shift from arrival thinking to legacy living. It's freedom, not obligation. We'll explore how gratitude works, and you'll notice a shift from an internal to an external focus.

Part 3 will help you subtly redefine success, integrate faith with action and discover the delight of opening doors for others.

There's nothing to memorize; you're still you. But you'll appreciate knowing "everything's good" with your drive train as you embark on the rest of your trip.

I'll tell personal and historic anecdotes to keep these concepts within reach. I'll explain concepts in easy-to-understand terms,

Turn today's 1440 minutes into momentum.
Download your free tracker at 1440Tracker.com

and each chapter will conclude with a lab with space to capture your thoughts and impressions. You're busy. This book isn't intended to bog you down. It's intended to lift your head, coax you to look farther out, and enjoy living with an abundance mindset.

> "My candle doesn't have to go out for another's to burn brightly." - Jaachynma N.E. Agu

INFLUENCED encourages us to light someone's flame from our own, or fan it so it burns brighter.

Please feel free to adapt what you read here. Customize what you discover to your context. I know I'm writing to bright, successful, busy people. These thoughts are presented sequentially and build as you read, but you don't have to read from the beginning to the end; please feel free to read as needed at any time.

The LAB at the end of each chapter is designed to help you stop and reflect. I encourage you to "Think a lot, write a little." Because transformation happens in reflection, if that's a new concept right now, hopefully you'll come to appreciate it in the first few chapters. Slow down. (How often do you hear *that* in the work week?) When you write, don't worry about polished prose; honest reflection is much better. If you need to free-write to get started, please do so.

Turn today's 1440 minutes into momentum.
Download your free tracker at 1440Tracker.com

If you and a few friends decide to read INFLUENCED as a group, you'll find the discussion will probably flow freely. Welcome learning from each other's insights and experience.

A Word About Faith

You'll see frequent mentions of faith and Scripture in the chapters that follow. There's one reason for that: it's part of who I am.
I know first-hand the tension we faith-driven professionals feel between marketplace success and spiritual significance.
It's frustrating at times and rewarding at others.

Legacy-Level Living is *not* a code word for abandoning your professional identity for full-time ministry. The marketplace desperately needs authentic integrity at every level. Be glad you're where you are and able to encourage your friends, family, and colleagues. One of the biggest challenges for some readers, maybe you, will be to weave your faith throughout your work week, because it's an integral part of who you are. Think integration, not compartmentalization.

If you're a non-faith reader, I hope you'll take a moment to read through. The principles we'll unwrap together work regardless, so stay with me, okay?

Let's wrap up this introduction with something my maternal Grandmother (Mom & Aunt Pauline's mom) said. She was originally from Oklahoma, and her "bless her heart" and other Southern idioms always made me smile:

"A hypocrite is someone who's not himself on Sunday."

Legacy-Level Living is consistent every day.

Turn today's 1440 minutes into momentum.
Download your free tracker at 1440Tracker.com

CHAPTER 1: You've Been Influenced!

"Ten Chimneys shares the back property line," Scott, the owner of the house we wanted to buy, told us. "No one will ever build back there; it's just been named a national historic site." When Ten Chimneys, the retirement estate of Broadway greats Alfred Lunt and Lynn Fontanne, was restored and opened to the public, I trained and began volunteering as a docent —a storytelling tour guide. Their lives and philosophy fascinated me. Still, there was SO much information to cram into each 2-hour tour, so I word smithed my tour, treating each room as a song on my playlist, and I'd customize it as my audience of 10 responded (or didn't) to the stories I told as we walked the grounds and toured the buildings. The Lunts officially or unofficially mentored scores of actors, actresses, neighborhood friends, and even family members throughout their long careers, and they often emphasized the importance of gratitude.

I decided it would be good, perhaps clever, to finish each of my tours by encouraging my small audience to think about who opened a gate or a door for them. "Who presented an opportunity that set you up for something good? Who encourages you? Call them when we get back to the Program Center. "Just wanted to say a quick thank you." Write them a note or a letter and thank them for the part they played in the script of your life." It was a sweet way to end the tour, with people reflecting on their lives in the shadow of these Broadway greats who lived so selflessly.

Turn today's 1440 minutes into momentum.
Download your free tracker at 1440Tracker.com

One day, it occurred to me. I've been influenced - and I've never told him so. I need to. So I started my letter. I called the office at Meeker High School in Meeker, Colorado, and discovered that a former classmate, Tom, was the current music teacher. He helped me find Mr. Jens's address, now in Grand Junction, Colorado. I finished my nice, long letter, not knowing how Mr. Jens' eyesight might be, enlarged the font, printed it off, and mailed it to him. There! He knows now. I can add that to my tours if it seems appropriate.

A few weeks later, I received a card from Grand Junction. The envelope was pink, the handwriting obviously feminine. "Oh no. I'm too late!" I thought. It was from Mrs. Jens. She wrote kindly of how much he enjoyed and appreciated the letter, and that they'd shared it with family and friends. One line especially made me smile. "He intends to answer your letter himself, but he's still the absent-minded professor we both remember, so we might all be surprised at when." Her thoughtful words encouraged me. I'd said Thank You and brightened his day. They're both gone now, but it's great to know I thanked Jens for his influence in my life while he was alive.

My letter to him is the first in this chapter's Case Stories.

Have you ever stopped to think about who shaped you? Most people haven't. We focus on what we've done, how we've worked, what we've built. But all of us are products of influence —shaped by people and experiences we don't always catalog or credit. We're quick to list achievements, but slow to list those who helped.

We're wired for earned pride —the story that we made ourselves. Especially for professionals, the "self-made" myth feels satisfying.

Turn today's 1440 minutes into momentum.
Download your free tracker at 1440Tracker.com

Yet acknowledging influence doesn't shrink what you've achieved. It puts it in context.

Here's an analogy: imagine you're driving a car through town. You steer, choose your course, and hit the brakes when needed. You earned your license. Yet someone taught you how to drive, someone owned the car you practiced in, and countless others engineered the roads, painted the lines, and hung the traffic lights. You get full credit for driving well. But you travel on infrastructure built by others.

Your success is solid. And the foundations underneath it—those are real too. Both truths live together. The more you notice how you were helped, the easier it becomes to help others on purpose.

Recognition always precedes replication. Until you recognize what you received, you'll struggle to give it back intentionally. If you want to become generous with your influence, the first step isn't action. It's inventory.

The Influence Inventory You Probably Haven't Taken

We talk a lot about mentorship and personal growth—less about the patches and pieces of influence we collect over decades. Some came directly, others through observation or proximity. Even negative experiences can shape us, pushing us toward things we might not have chosen.

Influence arrives in categories:

- **Direct influence**—those who coached, taught, or walked with you.
- **Indirect influence**—authors, speakers, neighbors, or public figures you never met.

- **Negative influence**—people who hurt you, adversities, losses and struggles; pain is a kind of influence.
- **Compound influence**—layers and echoes from different directions; maybe your mother and coach both instilled kindness, and you absorbed it from each source.

And then there's the principle of **lineage**. You might know it as the "Timothy principle." Timothy's story—his mother and grandmother instilling values, long before a mentor named Paul—reminds us that influence often comes from family, friends, or early relationships. Sometimes we don't realize who shaped us until years later, when their lessons surface at just the right time.

> Humility, seasoned by clarity, lets us trace our influences without self-deprecation. Acknowledging who molded us doesn't erase our own effort. It sharpens it.

That's the invitation: carry out your own influence inventory. For many, it's the first time. This inventory becomes your influence curriculum—your guide for shaping others effectively.

Legacy Lines That Shaped You

Influence doesn't sit still. It passes through lineages—some you know well, some you'd never think of tracing. Where did your leadership style come from? Probably not a single book. More likely, it emerged from observing someone handle tension, debrief a mistake, or build trust over time.

If you're a parent, you've watched legacy lines firsthand. Maybe you mirror your parents in some ways. Maybe you react against them in others. Either way, you've been influenced.

Four main channels set these legacy lines:

- **Character formation**—integrity, diligence, or compassion, caught from people who lived the life.
- **Skill development**—learning to think critically, write clearly, and solve problems, all modeled and honed through feedback.
- **Vision expansion**—seeing someone else break through permits you to imagine it's possible, too.
- **Pattern recognition**—watching mentors decode situations until you can read dynamics intuitively yourself.

Sometimes the impact compounds. Your grandmother's faith influences your mother's parenting, shapes your own values, and colors how you lead—three generations layered.

Two dangers come from ignoring legacy lines:

- **Arrogance:** The "self-made" myth insulates us from gratitude and dulls our effectiveness as leaders.
- **Blindness:** When you don't know how you were shaped, you miss the mechanics that can help you influence others now.

Legacy work isn't mystical. The mechanics are practical and transferable. If someone showed you, you can show someone else.

Why This Matters

Clarity is a gift. When you're close to the action, it can be challenging to see the patterns get lost. But if you intentionally pan back, the lines and trajectories begin to appear:

- The professor whose standards felt unreasonable?
  Now you see how they prepared you for complexity.

- The project that demanded everything?
  Maybe it was an investment in your growth.

- The friend who would rather risk comfort to speak truth?
  That was someone shaping your character, not passing judgment.

Intentional stewardship of wisdom, relationships, and resources isn't limited by age, even though you may have been led to believe it is. You can be for others what someone was for you if you've ever seen a 10-year-old soccer player show a teammate a cool technique that'll help them, or a high school or college musician show the person next to them an alternate fingering or bowing, you know what I mean.

This isn't about guilt ("I should give back"). It's stewardship ("How will I use what I've been given?"). Exhaustion comes from spending energy without clear direction—saying yes to good things that aren't really *your* things. When you inventory your influencers, you begin to discover your influence curriculum—the blueprint for how you're meant to shape others.

The ways you were shaped reveal ways you're equipped to shape others—not by cloning yourself, but by understanding the mechanics.

Turn today's 1440 minutes into momentum.
Download your free tracker at 1440Tracker.com

> Gratitude emerges as you name what you've received, and gratitude is what transforms both you and those you influence.

(We'll dig deeply into this in Chapter 4.)

From Recognition to Responsibility

Naming your influences is serious work—but it's not heavy. Responsibility isn't guilt. That distinction matters.

Guilt says you owe a debt you can never repay. Responsibility says you have something to steward.

You can't pay them back directly; the math doesn't work that way. Influence multiplies forward, not backward. Stewardship is the mindset: you pass the good of what you've received on to someone who needs it now.

Your influence inventory becomes your influence curriculum. The ways you were shaped mark the gifts you now carry. The doors that opened for you are the ones you're best equipped to open for another. This is not about obligation—it's about clarity.
It's not an extra task; it's about owning what influence you already possess, then directing it with intention.

Before we move ahead, pause with these three real questions (not rhetorical—not just "something to think about"):

Turn today's 1440 minutes into momentum.
Download your free tracker at 1440Tracker.com

1. **Who influenced you?**
2. **How did they shape you?**
3. **What did they give you that you're still using?**

Your journey is richer when you name these answers. You are the driver, but the roads beneath you were built long before you arrived. As you begin the next chapter, your influence story is clear—you didn't travel alone. And that truth, recognized, becomes the first page of your own legacy work.

Case Stories

Dale Jens - High School Music Teacher

Here's the letter I sent to Mr. Jens, 30 years after graduating from high school. He influenced me greatly and you'll see some of the above reflected in my letter.

Dear Mr. Jens,　　　　　　　　June 7, 2004

Recently I learned your approximate whereabouts from the current music teacher at Meeker High School. He said you were doing well and in good health so far as he knew, that you were playing in a community band and enjoying it. I hope he's right, even understating things a bit.

This letter is intended to encourage you. To thank you for your investment in my life some thirty years ago.

To let you know in my own words how much you influenced a young musician's life and shaped it. You helped create a "bent" in me that remains to this day.

Jens, as we called you, you profoundly influenced the "phil" in my philosophy in more than just a musical sense. I hope you don't mind that this is typed, and that the font is large. I want you to be able to read and re-read it, even after your eyes make new demands on you. I want you to be able to remember and smile, knowing that like Glen Holland in "Mr. Holland's Opus" you had a profound impact on your students, and like his students, yours are making their mark in the world. In part that is because of your example, your teaching, and your mentorship.

I hope the lines that follow spell "Thank You" in a way that brightens your smile every time you read them, bringing back some fond memories of your years at Meeker. I hope you know that for this one, and who knows how many others, you made a difference. Thank you.

I remember coming to Meeker half-way through my sophomore year. I had wanted to excel in athletics, particularly basketball, at the Nebraska school I came from. But I arrived too late in Meeker's basketball season to make the cut. I knew I couldn't wrestle. Not that I would have wanted to – wrestling looked like torture in 90-second increments! But I, of course, was in choir. We were preparing Fiddler on the Roof medley, and I noticed a cue line for violin. When I asked if you'd like me to work on it, maybe play next to Mary at the piano, I remember you smiling (probably wondering " who is this over-confident new kid anyway?"). I heard you say we were too close to concert to add anything new. "Let's not. What I do need, if you're interested, is a bass player in concert band." And you offered to send the bass and instruction books home with me over Christmas break so I could teach myself how to play that overgrown violin.

Knowing what I know now about teachers and students, your suggestion was masterful. You created both opportunity and test for me at that moment, in a way that wouldn't kill the concert band. I'd teach myself bass and if I was any good I'd be an addition. If I wasn't, the band could easily bury my unamplified sounds. Perfect. I learned the bass, began to play in band second semester, and came to love the instrument. I think we were both a little surprised when I eeked my way into Colorado All-State High School Band a year later. You took a chance on a new kid. You set him up to win if he applied himself. Thank you. The summer after graduation I bought my own electric bass, a little red Fender; I still

Turn today's 1440 minutes into momentum.
Download your free tracker at 1440Tracker.com

have it and I still play. I use your technique with promising students and I – like you – smile when they rise to the challenge.

I remember that you went with me to Greeley my first year in Colorado All-State High School Band – a junior and his band director. We attended a tuba and percussion recital. I'm not sure what your motivation was, maybe you knew one of the UNC profs. Perhaps you were in the mood for a bit of variety. Maybe the recital had been promoted by UNC's Music Department. Maybe it was something to do besides watch TV back at the room. (Those were the days when a director & student could share a room on a trip and no one thought twice about it – how times have changed!) I do know why *I* went – "Because Jens said 'Let's'." I had never seen anything like it before. So many sizes of tubas. Such skill. Such fun to be had! I didn't know *what* to say. And then the percussion recital followed. Mallets and sticks. Rhythm and melody. Precision so clean I wondered why we didn't *all* subdivide the beat. I was so impressed I had difficulty describing it when we got back to Meeker!

I remember the day I caught you for a second in your office off the band room and asked if you would teach me to conduct. You had me read a book from your shelf in preparation. Then another. Then a thick, technical text, DRY-as-dust. When I finally brought the last one back, read but hardly understood, you smiled. "You mean business, don't you?" (Apparently I passed the entrance exam to receive your tutoring.) You began to work with me. What you taught me between that moment and graduation sealed it in my thinking. *I love making music with groups of people!* I learned enough I could have tested out of my first semester of Conducting I. More importantly, you helped launch my career.

I watched how you worked with people so I could learn to do likewise. When you let me work first with a girls' chorus and then with the concert band, I knew you were giving me the opportunity to try my hand at what could become my livelihood. You mentored before "mentor" was a buzz-word in our society. Thank you.

I remember watching one of UNC's concert bands, sitting next to you in the bleachers. Dr. Wayman Walker walked into the gymnasium, bowed to acknowledge the audience's applause, and stepped onto the podium. With the band's every eye on him, his baton poised, I saw it. A single preparatory beat. With his down-beat the march began! But Dr. Walker only conducted the first measure! I watched a few seconds.

"Jens!" I turned to you, "he's not conducting!"

"Oh, yes he is," you whispered. "His work was all done in rehearsal. He'll just help them turn the corners. They – are prepared."

I was amazed. In the hour that followed, watching him and growing in my admiration for the band, it became clear; the band is not there for the conductor, the conductor is there for the band. When the group is skilled and prepared, he or she can become invisible. You set a paradigm for me, a way to measure my success, long before I knew paradigm was even in the dictionary.

I remember the trip you took to Walden, Colorado for a choral clinic and took Ron Bicknell, Tom Jirak and me with you. You had chosen a Jazz Gloria for their performance, so brought your rhythm section with you. I remember one thing about that trip. "This is _so much fun_! I love this!" It wasn't the getting out of class; it wasn't the travel. I don't remember if we stayed the night there

Turn today's 1440 minutes into momentum.
Download your free tracker at 1440Tracker.com

or not. I just remember we did our best to stay right with you so you could work with the singers, and not have to stop for us. In the concert you directed, at the end of our song, I breathed a little prayer. *This is what I want to do with my life, God. May I?* He said "yes." and my life has been spent working with people, leading, directing, guiding and helping.

I enjoy telling groups the last part of a story that includes you. It was the year we went to Colorado Springs as a band to play for the CMEA (Colorado Music Educators Association). We were accustomed to bringing I's home from contest, and while we sat waiting quietly for the activity in front of the curtain to conclude (we were next), you gave us a curtain talk. I can still hear your words. You reminded us "The people out there are not aunts, uncles and grandparents who don't know any different. They are music teachers. Every – last – one – of – them." (You said it slowly and let it sink in, I remember.) "You know these songs. You play them well. Pay attention, please, follow me close, and let's do these so well, those music teachers out there forget to critique our performance and instead just enjoy it. Shall we?" We nodded yes. Then you smiled a little and shrugged. "Besides, we've already gotten "Ones" on a couple of these." I wove that concept into my philosophy. I have endeavored these years to have "my" groups always play and sing with excellence enough to free the critical listener. I want musicians to forget to critique and instead allow themselves to be encouraged by what we do. I first learned it from you.

That same weekend I was somewhere in your shadow while people milled around before or after an event at CMEA.

Turn today's 1440 minutes into momentum.
Download your free tracker at 1440Tracker.com

I overheard a colleague ask you what you do to get 110 kids from a small mountain town to play so well. A regimen? Something to do with the high altitude? A diet perhaps? A curriculum? Your answer surprised me. But it made perfect sense. "Actually, the secret to my success at the high school is a person. She's here somewhere. Her name is Mary Villa and she starts my kids out in elementary school and has them through junior high. My incoming freshmen have already played high school literature. I can just keep on building. That's what enables us to play college and professional literature."

And we did. I recall one time you handed me a hand-written part and asked me to put it on a 3rd clarinet stand on stage where the band was set up. When I asked you about it, you vented a little (not too much) and assured me we *would* be playing that song in concert on Friday night. "I *will* challenge my best players," you said. "I have first trumpets who can play. Really play. This song was a stretch for them, and they got it." I knew you were talking about Tom, who later succeeded you at Meeker (and helped me find you), your son Dan, and Debbie. "If I have to," you continued, "I will re-write a part for third clarinet players who can't –or won't– practice. But my best players *will* play and be challenged."

Just one more, then I'll stop. You may remember that I used to listen to publishers' demo recordings when they came to the school. When I noticed something special, I'd make a note for when you previewed them later. One of your comments has endured, spanning three decades of my own music screening. I motioned you over toward the stereo one day as you strode into the room. I had been listening to new tunes. "Jens, come listen. This is really neat."

Turn today's 1440 minutes into momentum.
Download your free tracker at 1440Tracker.com

You stopped and folded your arms in front of you while I played it for you.

A catchy little motif came over the speakers one wave after another. After a while you began to shake your head. "Awww, why not, Jens? That's a neat riff!"

"That it is, but that's all it is. See?" And you took thirty seconds to show me what you meant. "See, Phil? He wrote eight measures, but he's trying to get credit for thirty-two. No sale." Then you smiled as you turned toward your office. "Don't ever do that." Somehow I think you knew I wouldn't. That moment was my introduction to Form and Analysis.

Well, I hope you have enjoyed these anecdotes; each incident taught me a concept I've used my entire career. I just wanted to tell you how thankful I am for the years I had you as my teacher, model and mentor. You shaped my life more than you knew – until today.

Last year I went through the training and qualified to be a docent for the Ten Chimneys Foundation (literally in my back yard), the estate of Broadway greats, Alfred Lunt and Lynn Fontanne. I conclude each of my tours emphasizing the people in their lives – the mentors they had and the actors and actresses they inspired and mentored. Last year I said, "If I ever learn the whereabouts of my high school band and choir director, I'm going to write him a long letter. I don't think he knows how much he influenced my life." This year I can say, "I found him, wrote him a long letter, and I hope it made his day." Then I will encourage my guests to write or call someone who made a difference for them as they grew up, and invest in a youngster who shows promise. "You never know

Turn today's 1440 minutes into momentum.
Download your free tracker at 1440Tracker.com

who they might become. Be generous when you invest in the next generation."

I wish you good health and happy days, Mr. Jens – Dale.

You have been, and are, one of my heroes.

Thanks for taking a chance on a sophomore new-kid.

Thanks for agreeing to teach a junior how to conduct.

Thanks for giving a senior a taste of what it might be like to make a career of this "arts" thing. I love it.

And I'm doing my best to pass the baton to others who will carry it well.

You are the first to read these paragraphs, and that is as it *should* be. They will one day be adapted and placed as a tribute to you on my website. People frequently ask about the people who have shaped my thinking. As my protege's and other interested people read these paragraphs, and others, I hope they will be encouraged and challenged. Perhaps they will even copy some of the things we've done right along the way!

With deep and sincere appreciation,
(and I signed it)

Meeker High School – Class of 1974

PS. Did we ever tell you the origin of "Legato Half-note," the affectionate nickname a half-a-dozen of us had for you? Several of us were sitting along the windows in the school lobby one morning before class, and our sponsor, Mrs. Stoddard, walked by. High-heels. Short, quick steps. "Those are staccato eighth-notes," we agreed. We measured the sound of her heels on the tile floor till she turned into the office. Not long after, you strolled by.

Much taller. Not in a hurry. You waved good morning, and we smiled and waved back. I noticed your gait that morning and said, "those are not staccato eighth-notes". "Nope, those are half-notes," someone said. And Tom Bement (trombone player) said in his dramatic way,

"Le-ga-to". From that day on, in our little group, you were Legato Half-note. Always with respect, always reminding us – don't hurry so much. Enjoy life. Like Jens does.

Jerry Price, College Professor

Jerry Price travelled with the summer touring group I was in for a couple of weeks, during my second year with the group. I'd found myself "between a rock and a hot plate" the previous week and needed some guidance. As we rode along in the van I asked for his perspective and counsel. He could have shared his opinion, but instead, he took me to 1 Samuel 30. David and his troops had been out doing what they believed was the right thing to do, but when they returned to Ziklag, the place was in smoldering ruin, their wives and children all gone. Then David's men turn on him too. Jerry pointed to verse eight. "Ask God what to do, Phil. David didn't turn to his wife, she'd been taken captive. And you don't have one," he smiled. "He didn't write a new song. Who knows, his instruments may have been stolen. He went straight to the Lord and asked ' What shall I do?'"

"Listen," he told me, "Ask God straight-out – 'Shall I do this?'

As soon as He confirms it in your thinking, go after it. Go after it <u>hard</u>." I can still hear the way he said "go after it hard." – like he'd coach a point guard on his basketball team; same tone of

Turn today's 1440 minutes into momentum.
Download your free tracker at 1440Tracker.com

voice. Then he took me to verse 18. "Look what it says. David recovered it all. Not one thing was lost. If you do what the Lord tells you – it'll take work, but you can recover everything. Everything."

I can't tell you how many times I've revisited 1 Samuel 30 over the decades. I had the chance several years later to thank him for his guidance. My "Thank you!" warmed his heart and brought a smile.

Mrs. Siemering, 8th-Grade Teacher.

First semester, I was one of 500 8th graders at East Junior High School, Aurora, Colorado. My family moved in January.

Second semester, I was one of 2 8th graders at Tallin School, a one-room K-8 country school 14 miles from Arnold, Nebraska.

I survived the transition! My classmate, Becky, and I joked that we were either top of the class or bottom of the class, and that could change on Friday when Mrs. Siemering averaged this week's grades. I loved my country school experience. I didn't mind at all being in the same room as my Kindergarten and 2nd-grade sisters. And for a 13 year-old, that's saying something.

Mrs. Siemering had two profound effects on my life, from which I benefit to this day.

Soon after my arrival, she noticed I was taking homework with me at night. She motioned me to her desk at the front of the room one morning and privately let me know that wasn't necessary if I used my time wisely during the day.

"Really?" I was intrigued. What kid wouldn't jump at the chance to live homework-free? Especially a city kid who figured it was expected.

She smiled and gave me a couple of hints.

1) Don't put up with clutter. If you know where everything is and there's nothing extra in your desk, it won't take you as long to get started on an assignment.
2) Tune out what's happening here at the front of the room until your assignments are done. Then listen in if you want.

Quiet woman that she was, I still remember the morning not long after, when she saw my family arrive and we three kids climbed out of our VW bug carrying only our lunchboxes. She looked at my empty left hand and then caught my eye. Her *No books, hmm?* smile arrived without a word, but I felt her approval. Those new disciplines soon became part of my everyday routine, enabling me to focus at my desk while other students did their recitations up front. Clutter went away. I didn't take homework home the rest of the year, and to this day I name Tallin School as where I learned to study.

I remember also, her summoning me to her desk near the end of the school year. "Phil, I'd like a moment with you." She reviewed with me the quarter's progress and assured me mine would be a good report card. Then she took a deep breath and pointed to the penmanship section of the card. "This..." she paused. "Penmanship. Phil, yours is terrible. Unfortunately for me, but luckily for you, it's too late for me to do anything about it." It took a second, but I caught a hint of her smile out of the corner of my eye. "Next year you'll have one elective as a Freshman, and I suggest you take Typing I. By typing your papers, you'll avoid negative reactions from your teachers when you turn in reports. You might earn higher marks, who knows? Are you interested?"

I was 13; she was a mature adult with what seemed like a solid recommendation. "Ummm, sure." We finished my review and I went back to my desk.

The next week she motioned me to the front again. "I've spoken with Mrs. Tryon, and while having Freshmen in Typing 1 is not the norm, she understands my recommendation and you'll be in her class in the Fall." It wasn't until I was back at my desk that I realized: Suzanne, Johnny-Mike and Sarah attend here. Mrs. Tryon was their grandmother. No wonder that happened fast.

On Sunday at church, Mrs. Tryon made a point of speaking to me. "I'm so glad you're going to be in my class this Fall," she smiled, "Looking forward to it." Yep, the ladies had talked.

I got A's in Typing I. First, on the manual typewriters, then on the electrics. I began to type my papers on Dad's Royal manual typewriter. My first week at college I bought myself a little blue Smith Corona electric with a manual carriage return, since it was cheaper than the electric return and Consumer Reports said it would last longer. My profs never complained about my poor penmanship. They hardly ever saw my writing.

What would Mrs. Siemering say if she knew that today, as a professional writer, I live with QWERTY under my left fingertips and type faster than I can write?

Her quiet, unassuming gift of good advice in those few months. First, how to study. Second, "Please, take Typing I." She changed my life.

Turn today's 1440 minutes into momentum.
Download your free tracker at 1440Tracker.com

LAB: Recognition & Response

Thinking Shift:

From: "I've achieved this through my own talent and hard work."

To: "My achievements are real AND built on foundations others laid for me."

Key Insight:
Acknowledging influence doesn't diminish your achievement. It clarifies your responsibility and reveals your curriculum for influencing others.

ACTION: The Influence Inventory

Step 1: Map Your Influencers (20 minutes)

Create four lists identifying people who shaped you:

- **Direct Influencers**
Teachers, mentors, and coaches who intentionally invested in you.

_____

_____

_____

_____

_____

- **Indirect Influencers**
People you observed and learned from (bosses, colleagues, family members)

_____

_____

_____

_____

- **Negative Influencers**
People whose example showed you what NOT to do (still shaped you)

_____

_____

_____

_____

- **Compound Influencers**
People who influenced your influencers or whose influence combined with others to have an impact (generational impact).

_____

_____

Step 2: Identify Your Legacy Lines (15 minutes)

For your top 3-5 influencers, answer:

• What specific quality, skill, or perspective did they give you?

_____

_____

_____

• Are you still using it today? How?

_____

_____

_____

• Where in your current influence are you replicating what they gave you?

_____

_____

_____

Step 3: Choose One Expression (This week)

Select one person from your list and express gratitude specifically:

• Write a letter (even if you can't send it)
• Make a phone call
• Share their influence with someone they impacted through you

_____

_____

_____

Turn today's 1440 minutes into momentum.
Download your free tracker at 1440Tracker.com

Checkpoint Milestone:

❑ *I can name at least 10 people who significantly shaped who I am, and I've thanked at least one of them specifically.*

Scriptural Footings

On Recognizing Influence & Legacy Lines:

- 2 Timothy 1:3-5 – Timothy's faith lineage
- Proverbs 13:22 – Generational inheritance
- 1 Corinthians 4:15-17 – Paul and Timothy
- Deuteronomy 6:6-9 – Passing down faith

On Gratitude & Acknowledgment:

- 1 Thessalonians 5:18 – Thankfulness in everything
- Colossians 3:15 – Let peace rule
- Psalm 100:4 – Enter with thanksgiving
- Philippians 1:3-5 – Grateful remembrance

On Humility & Recognition:

- 1 Corinthians 4:7 – What do you have that you didn't receive?
- James 1:17 – Every good gift
- Proverbs 27:2 – Let others praise
- Romans 12:3 – Sober self-assessment

On Being Shaped for Purpose:

- Jeremiah 18:1-6 – Potter and clay
- Ephesians 2:10 – Created for good works
- Psalm 139:13-16 – Fearfully and wonderfully made

Turn today's 1440 minutes into momentum.
Download your free tracker at 1440Tracker.com

34

Turn today's 1440 minutes into momentum.
Download your free tracker at 1440Tracker.com

CHAPTER 2: Hidden Mentors

It was late summer, 1978. Brenda and I had just returned from a candidating interview for a ministry position in eastern Nebraska that didn't go well. We knew within the first hour there that we were not what the church needed, but finished the weekend even though we'd already decided no-thanks. We had car trouble on the return trip that kept us a night in Chicago (with extended family, fortunately), and a flat tire on the Michigan interstate the next morning. It didn't help that the spare was super low on air too! We finally arrived at home about noon on Monday, and I, needing to gain some sense of accomplishment decided to go to work for the afternoon. The office was within walking distance so I left the car where it sat. *I'll tend to you after work.* I wasn't to the end of the block, when our phone rang. It was the pastor of a church in western Nebraska that I'd respected —ok, admired— for years. Friends had helped start the church and I loved when our family got to visit.

"You just missed him. He'll be back a little after five," Brenda told him. Mom and Dad had been with the Bonds' over the weekend and in getting caught up on what each other's kids were doing, they'd discovered that Calvary Memorial, the Bonds' growing church, was looking for two new pastors, one of them music & youth, and I was a recent graduate looking for a full-time position. He called again after work to describe what they were looking for and see if I was interested. I was!

Turn today's 1440 minutes into momentum.
Download your free tracker at 1440Tracker.com

"We have a board meeting tonight, I'll be sure to mention you. Can you mail me your resume tomorrow?" he asked.

"I'm a recent graduate, but sure. It'll include student accomplishments, and I'll include the phone number of the pastor that oversaw my internship in Muskegon, in case you'd like to talk to him." This was before the days of the personal computer and email, remember.

The next evening after work I received another phone call from Pastor Bonds. The news was surprisingly good. Several of the men on the church board knew my family and me, respected my parents' ministry and my musicianship. They planned to present my name as the candidate for Music & Youth at a special business meeting – a week from Sunday!

"Do you need to come visit? Does Brenda need to come see? If not, we're ready to vote a week from Sunday." Wide-eyed in near disbelief, I covered the mouthpiece and asked her. Her smile beaming, she said, 'I guess not; this is definitely the Lord's doing.'

"She said no," I answered, "The Lord is definitely in this."

In one congregational meeting, Calvary Memorial transitioned from having one pastor to having three. They called me as Music & Youth Pastor, and Dennis as Outreach Pastor. I'd been friends with his family since childhood.

When we drove up in our U-Haul, Pastor drove us to see two places to rent. One in town, one in the country.

We chose the one in the country and went to get the truck. Pastor made a couple of phone calls, and a few men came to help. We were unloaded and moved in before dark, and the church paid our first month's rent.

I'm humbled each time I recount how that all transpired. My parents' life and ministry had a significant impact on my calling. While I grew up just trying to stay out of trouble in my early years, they poured themselves into me. Taught me right from wrong. Excellence from so-so. Principles. Discipline. Winsomeness. And they had enough confidence in me to speak up when they learned about a place I could probably do well. I'm so glad they did.

We enjoyed a fruitful season of ministry there. Four years later, we remodeled the platform to accommodate the choirs during our festivals. Of the church's 400 regular attenders, 140 of them were in children's, youth, and adult choirs!

The Invisible Influence Network

How much of your story happened beyond your awareness? Most influence operates below the surface, like the mass of an iceberg under the waterline. You see your own effort, but beneath it lies an unseen network of people who prayed, advocated, modeled, and built systems that made your achievement possible.

If you trace the story of how you arrived where you are, the honest version includes more than your own choices. It includes opportunities you didn't create, conversations in rooms you never entered, people praying when you didn't know you needed prayer, and systems built by individuals you've never met.

Recognizing this isn't about diminishing your effort. You've worked hard, made sacrifices, and persisted when others gave up.

But it's equally valid that your work rested on foundations built by others.

The self-made myth is problematic for two reasons.

First, it breeds entitlement: believing you built everything by yourself makes you less grateful and more defensive about your success.

Second, it blocks you from becoming a hidden mentor yourself. If you don't see how others shaped your path, you won't recognize when it's your turn to quietly shape someone else's.

Authentic leadership—what I call *Legacy-Level Living*—means investing invisibly. It's not about platform. It's about offering the same quiet gifts others once gave you, whether or not anyone ever knows.

Categories of Hidden Influencers

The Intercessors:
Those Who Prayed When You Didn't Know

Somewhere in your past, someone prayed for you. A grandparent who asked God to guide your steps. A parent carrying your name through years you didn't deserve it. A spiritual mentor who interceded quietly while you were distracted elsewhere.

You can't measure this kind of influence. You can't diagram causation. But anyone of faith knows the compound effect of steady prayer across years can be profound.

You may be someone's hidden intercessor now, praying for your children, your team, your pastor, your clients. They may never know, but heaven does.

Honoring unseen prayer cultivates humility and gratitude, the twin foundations of sustainable influence.

The Door-Openers:
Those Who Created Opportunities You Didn't Know Existed

Every career turning point has invisible fingerprints on it. Someone mentioned your name in a meeting. Someone vouched for you when you weren't there. Someone said, "She's ready," and opened a door you didn't even know existed.

These advocates spend relational capital on your behalf. Sometimes they see potential you don't yet recognize. Sometimes they pay forward what someone once did for them.

Ask yourself: How much of what I've built depended on unseen advocates? And how can I now open doors for others without needing credit for it? The most powerful advocacy often happens in rooms where your name is mentioned and you aren't present. That's not a problem—that's influence working exactly as it should.

The Model-Makers:
Those Who Showed You a Pattern Without Teaching It

Not all mentors teach intentionally. Some influence simply by living well within your sightline. A supervisor's calm under fire. A parent's steady grace in hardship. A business leader's integrity when cutting corners seemed easier.

These models normalize a higher standard. They show what balance looks like, what faithfulness can feel like, what quiet competence can achieve.

Turn today's 1440 minutes into momentum.
Download your free tracker at 1440Tracker.com

You didn't take notes at the time, but their pattern imprinted. And years later, when faced with a similar moment, you instinctively responded as they once did.

Think of whose life gave you permission to grow into who you've become. Then ask—who is quietly watching me now, without my awareness, learning how to lead by how I live?

The Preparation-Makers:
Those Who Built Systems You Inherited

Almost every advantage you enjoy sits atop invisible scaffolding. The founder who built the organization you joined. The teacher who shaped the curriculum you now master. The reformer who fought uphill battles so your work could even exist in the open.

Systems feel ordinary when they're working, so we forget they were once someone's fight. Yet our lives flow within structures others built—educational systems, workplace cultures, legal freedoms, even family rhythms. These preparation-makers constructed the foundations from which we now launch.

Gratitude for these unseen builders fights entitlement and reframes leadership.

> Your job isn't only to succeed within what exists, but to strengthen what future generations will inherit.

Turn today's 1440 minutes into momentum.
Download your free tracker at 1440Tracker.com

Why We Miss Hidden Mentors

Four forces make our hidden mentors easy to overlook.

Proximity bias. We remember influences that are close and visible but overlook those far away or indirect.

Timing blindness. Influence often precedes awareness by years. We appreciate a teacher at 35 for something they said at 15—long after they've moved on.

Attribution error. We credit success to effort but label others' contribution as "luck" or "breaks."

Spiritual amnesia. Even people of faith forget the invisible orchestration of providence when outcomes finally arrive.

The deeper danger isn't mere ingratitude. It's misunderstanding how influence actually works. If you assume only visibility equals impact, you'll chase recognition instead of legacy.

Seeing your hidden mentors changes how you operate. You pray for people who'll never know. You open doors quietly. You model integrity even when unseen. You build systems that outlast you. Influence becomes less about spotlight and more about stewardship.

The Practice of Remembrance

Remembering hidden mentors is not nostalgia; it's a deliberate spiritual discipline.

It dismantles entitlement by forcing you to face how many people helped you thrive.

It cultivates generosity because when you see how much you've received invisibly, you naturally want to invest the same way.

It nurtures humility—not false modesty, but honest recognition that you did not create success alone.

Practicing remembrance is simple. Regularly ask:

> Who prayed for me?
>
> Who opened doors for me?
>
> Who modeled something I've quietly replicated?

You won't know all the names—and that's the point. It trains your attention to see the invisible, and to become it. You are likely influencing someone right now who won't recognize your investment until years from now, if ever. That's not a flaw. That's the beauty of how sustained influence works.

Legacy-level influence isn't about being remembered; it's about remembering what made you who you are, then passing it forward in kind.

Case Stories

Stu Booth, Camp Counselor

In my growing-up years, mom and dad pastored Aurora Bible Church just east of Denver in the suburb of Aurora, Colorado, and at that church, Camp ID-RA-HA-JE, on the East slope of the Colorado Rockies, was the summer camp of choice. ID-RA-HA-JE was short for the founder & director's favorite song, I'd Rather Have Jesus.

I, of course, went willingly each year. The summer after my 7th-grade year (a less-than-stellar year), as we were getting settled, I met Stu, my counsellor for the week. Stu was a coaching major, here for the summer. In our first cabin meeting late that Sunday afternoon, Stu turned in surprise and pointed to the back of the cabin door. "Would you guys look at that?" He said, "Some idiot left a schedule taped to the back of the door. We know what they're going to say on the intercom and when. Can you believe that?" Our eyes widened. He had us where he wanted us. Then, as though he was thinking, he paused and looked at a couple of us. "That means we know what's coming next. (He paused.) If we do this right, we'll already be doing what they tell us to do when they come on the intercom to tell us to do something." We were intrigued now.

"Would you guys be interested in going all week without anybody telling you what to do when?"

Of course! It was unanimous, and we didn't even have to vote.

Then he said, "Here's what let's do. I'll ask, 'What time is it?' Whoever's closest to the door will find that time and read the next thing.

Turn today's 1440 minutes into momentum.
Download your free tracker at 1440Tracker.com

And we'll get a jump on it. When they tell us to clean our cabin in the mornings, we'll be almost done. We will be first in line for breakfast, lunch, and dinner, 'cuz we'll already be on our way to the dining hall when they come on the intercom to tell us it's time to go. . . . What do you think?"

We were all-in and we were great! The whole week went that way. We loved finishing before neighboring cabins when it was time to sweep up and clean up every day. We had our pick of where to sit in class. We were first or almost first for meals all week. Stu was right. Nobody told us what to do. All he had to say was "What time is it?" And we took it from there. It was beautiful. The best week of camp. Ever.

What I didn't realize until after camp was that I had just lived obediently for five days in a row — and I liked it. I brought that approach home with me and lived that same way because I knew what Mom and Dad were probably going to ask me to do next, and I just ...kind of... started early.

Mom told me years later that she and Dad sat at the kitchen table a couple of weeks after I got back from camp to redesign their approach to this discipline thing, because I was no longer the problem I had been before.

Stuart Booth changed my life in that week of camp. I'm pretty sure now that it was by design. But he helped me discover that living obediently is cool. It's too bad Jonah didn't know that. I don't know where Stu is these days. He may be in glory for all I know. But he changed my life.

Roger Rose, College Prof, Vocal Coach, Mentor

As a freshman music major at Grand Rapids School of the Bible and Music (we said Griz-boom), I was assigned a faculty rep to go to for anything related to my major. Roger Rose was mine. He was a pastor, the music department chairman, and my voice coach. We got along well. He taught me many things, for one, about attentiveness.

I noticed that whenever I stepped into his office, he always capped his pen and set it down. (His was a Parker pen like the president used at that time.) I knew I had his undivided attention. I can remember him saying, when I asked him about it, "As long as this pen is uncapped, I have thoughts in my brain trying to get to this legal pad. But if I cap the pen, it helps me focus on you."

I also remember coming in off my second year of touring with the school's summer touring group, and saying, "Mr. Rose, it seems like the last half of the tour or so I've wanted to stay behind to help some of the things these host churches say they're working on, things they're trying to do. Is that normal? To want to stay behind like that?"

He smiled and said, "I think probably what's happening is that the Lord has been preparing your heart to step into church ministry." A pastor near Muskegon has been calling me lately. "Don't you have somebody that you can send to help us with the music?"

After speaking with him, Mr. Rose proposed a two-year internship rather than just my senior year. He would supervise both. The second year, I would receive a grade for it, as per the music curriculum, but the first year would be for me to gain experience, help this church grow, and mature through on-the-job training.

It was a very successful two years, and I learned much from Pastor and Mrs. Saucer.

When my fiancé, Brenda, and I wanted to get married only 2 weeks after graduation, we asked Mr. Rose to lead us through pre-marital counselling, fulfilling that prerequisite for the officiating pastor in her home church.

Roger Rose helped set the trajectory for my entire ministry in the worship arts, connected me at the outset with a compassionate pastor to work under, and he helped us begin our marriage on the right foot. He invested in both of us.

LAB: Discovering Invisible Influence

Thinking Shift:

From: "I know who influenced me."

To: "There are people whose influence I've never recognized, and God orchestrated more than I've acknowledged."

Key Insight: The most powerful influence often happens invisibly. Recognizing hidden mentors trains you to become one.

ACTION: The Hidden Mentor Hunt

Step 1: Ask the Four Questions (15 minutes)

Reflect and journal:

1. The Intercessors: Who prayed for me when I didn't know? (parents, grandparents, church members, mentors' mentors)

_____

_____

_____

2. The Door-Openers: Who created opportunities I didn't see being created? (recommendations written, introductions made, advocacy in rooms I wasn't in)

_____

_____

Turn today's 1440 minutes into momentum.
Download your free tracker at 1440Tracker.com

3. The Model-Makers: Who showed me a pattern without teaching it? (how to handle conflict, lead with integrity, balance work and family)

_____

_____

_____

4. The Preparation-Makers: Who built systems/structures I inherited? (organizational cultures, family traditions, spiritual foundations)

_____

_____

_____

Step 2: Trace One Hidden Influence Line (20 minutes)

Choose one discovery from Step 1 and trace it:

• How did their invisible investment shape specific outcomes in your life?

_____

_____

_____

• What doors opened because of their behind-the-scenes work?

_____

_____

_____

- Who else benefited from what they built?

_____

_____

Step 3: Practice Hidden Mentoring (This month)

Intentionally do ONE hidden mentor action:
- Pray consistently for someone without telling them
- Write a recommendation or make an introduction
- Advocate for someone in a room they're not in
- Build something that will serve people you'll never meet

_____

_____

_____

Checkpoint Milestone:
❏ *I've identified at least 3 hidden mentors and taken one invisible action on behalf of someone else.*

Turn today's 1440 minutes into momentum.
Download your free tracker at 1440Tracker.com

Scriptural Footings

On God's Invisible Providence:
- Esther 4:14 – For such a time
- Genesis 50:20 – God meant it for good
- Romans 8:28 – Works together for good
- Proverbs 16:9 – The Lord directs

On Intercessory Prayer:
- Colossians 4:12 – Epaphras wrestling in prayer
- 1 Samuel 12:23 – Samuel's commitment to pray
- Job 42:10 – Job prayed for friends
- Romans 8:26-27 – Spirit intercedes

On Unseen Service:
- Matthew 6:3-4 – Don't let left hand know
- Colossians 3:23-24 – Work for the Lord
- 1 Corinthians 3:6-8 – Some plant, some water
- Hebrews 6:10 – God remembers your work

On Building for Others:
- 1 Corinthians 3:10-15 – Building on the foundation
- Nehemiah 2:18 – Let's start rebuilding
- Psalm 78:4-7 – Tell the next generation
- 2 Timothy 2:2 – Entrust to faithful people

CHAPTER 3: Arrival vs. Legacy

Our family visited Dad and Mom in New Mexico for a week over Father's Day 2002. Our only disappointment that week was having to come home early from one of our outings to a pueblo because Dad had a severe headache. Other than that, things went fine. It was a great vacation.

Dad received a diagnosis on July 7th, three weeks after our trip, that shocked us all. Glioblastoma. Stage four.

Dad passed away at home on August 2nd, less than hour after my flight from Wisconsin arrived.

Mom came to me privately not long after his passing, and gingerly asked if I would have his memorial service. I thought for a moment, and quietly answered that while it would be the hardest thing I'd ever done, it would also be an incredible honor, "I will," I said.

Dad and Mom weren't wealthy. They didn't even own a home until later in life. His churches were comparatively small, but he and Mom poured themselves into the people they were called to serve. Their friendships spanned miles and decades. At that funeral and afterward, I saw the outpouring of love and support from the people they had worked with and served over the years in Colorado, Nebraska, Wyoming, South Dakota, and most recently, New Mexico, where Mom was from.

Turn today's 1440 minutes into momentum.
Download your free tracker at 1440Tracker.com

The conversations and recollections that day went on and on:

> Pastor this....
> Dick & Shirley that...
> I remember how he...
> Remember when they...?

If there had ever been a doubt, I knew then for sure, that Dad and Mom had it right. People are your best investment.

First Grandpa - and I, in my 20s, resolved to carry on his legacy.
  And now Dad - two decades later.
  I will. People are my best investment.

The Arrival Illusion

Have you ever chased a finish line that kept moving? Maybe you reached a milestone, celebrated briefly, then immediately asked, "What's next?" It happens quietly. A new level, new number, new recognition, then the rush wears off and the treadmill restarts. Again.

Most professionals "arrive" multiple times. They hit career goals, earn new titles, cross income thresholds, build reputations, buy the bigger house, then the cabin, or launch their own brand. Each arrival feels big in its moment. It satisfies for a while. Then it the new becomes normal. Again.

The arrival illusion is the idea that there's a finish line where fulfillment finally stays put. We can smile, sigh in relief, and relax.

Arrival moments matter. Of course they do. They mark growth, discipline, and perseverance. But they're not destinations, they're milestones on a much longer road.

Turn today's 1440 minutes into momentum.
Download your free tracker at 1440Tracker.com

> Arrival is evidence of progress, but it's not proof of purpose.
>
> *(Read that sentence again.)*

At some point, if you're honest, a quiet question surfaces: "Is this all there is?"

That question doesn't signal failure. It signals that success alone isn't enough. Ironically, that ache shows up *after* a measure of success.

Arrival disappoints because it centers on you.
Your achievement, your recognition, your security.
Legacy satisfies because it centers on others.
Your contribution, their transformation. Shared fulfillment.

Chances are you've already mastered arrival. You've learned how to set goals, pursue them, and deliver results.
That mastery isn't wasted. It's preparation.
If arrival builds your platform;
legacy determines what you do with it.

Legacy-Level Living simply shifts the question
from "What have I achieved?" to "What have I contributed?"
Legacy-Level Living isn't abandoning ambition, it's redirecting it.
Ambition becomes the fuel for impact, rather than accumulation.

Choosing legacy doesn't mean your previous goals were wrong. You've proven you can arrive.

Turn today's 1440 minutes into momentum.
Download your free tracker at 1440Tracker.com

> The greater question is: what will you build that outlasts you?

Those who thrive over the long haul are those who learn to redirect achievement toward contribution.

> The reward isn't in arriving anymore. It's in investing.

Redefining Success: From Performance to Impact

Traditional measurements of success make perfect sense in early and middle career stages—title, income, recognition, stability. They're understandable and useful. But they're not sufficient for lasting satisfaction & fulfillment because they measure what you've accumulated, not what you've contributed.

After a while, that imbalance starts to show. You sense there's more to success than performance reviews and metrics. Legacy reframes success through impact questions instead:

Turn today's 1440 minutes into momentum.
Download your free tracker at 1440Tracker.com

> Who did you develop?
> What did you build that will outlast you?
> Whose potential did you help unlock?
> What doors did you open for others?

These questions don't make your performance irrelevant; they reveal indicators about your purpose:

> Your competence created the capacity for influence.
> Your resources created means for generosity.
> Your platform created opportunities for others to grow.
> Your wisdom created currency you can invest in others.

Consider two leaders reaching retirement at the same event.

The first lists achievements: awards, projects, growth percentages. The audience applauds politely.

The second talks about people: those they mentored, leaders they promoted, teams they helped flourish. The room feels different—warmth replaces applause.

One leader built results. The other built people who keep building.

Both were successful. Only one left successors.

ROI² The Return on Invested Influence

Most of us have learned to evaluate life through

ROI—Return on Investment.

Is my financial investment paying off? We add to, or move our investments depending on the ROI we're seeing.

Many of us also consider the

ROE—Return on Effort.

Am I investing my limited energy where it produces the greatest good?

We stop doing things that feel like a waste of time & energy. We pour ourselves into activities that pay off. It might be a side hustle, it might be the health club. It might be our volunteering. Great ROE? Stay committed and re-up.

Legacy-level thinking introduces a third measure:

ROI²—Return on Invested Influence.

It asks what others have gained
> through you,
> from you, or
> because they were near you.

Stop reading a second and consider that.

All three forms of measurement matter, but that third one turns success into legacy.

You can use it as a quick gauge:

✓ This opportunity—will it help me arrive or help me contribute?

✓ This investment—will it increase my security or my impact?

Turn today's 1440 minutes into momentum.
Download your free tracker at 1440Tracker.com

✓ This relationship—am I extracting value or creating value?

None of this is either/or thinking. It's both/and with reordered priorities. You've already arrived. You've built enough security and credibility to make selective, legacy-centered choices.

For some readers, the security piece is still evolving—and that's fine. You don't have to wait for perfect conditions to think legacy. Even while building, you can steer decisions toward contribution.

Legacy isn't something you start after success; it's how you define success from now on.

The pruning principle in John 15:2 puts this in context: God prunes productive branches to make them even more fruitful. His aim: Much fruit. What feels like restriction or loss—retirement, health changes, reduced visibility—might actually be redirection toward higher-yield fruit.

What if your current limitations aren't punishments but invitations to work at a longer time horizon, one that measures impact through others' growth? You may have heard it called "The Long Game."

Paul's advice to his protege, Timothy will serve you well too. "You have heard me teach things that have been confirmed by many reliable witnesses. Now teach these truths to other trustworthy people who will be able to pass them on to others."

(2 Timothy 2.2 NLT)

Your Influence Multiplied

Arrival measures what you produced.
Legacy measures what others continue to produce because of you.

Turn today's 1440 minutes into momentum.
Download your free tracker at 1440Tracker.com

The Great Commission said, "Go and make disciples." It didn't stop at converts; it envisioned people who reproduce influence in others.

Discipleship is influence multiplication—an exponential pattern where your investment ripples far beyond your direct reach. I like the term Disciple-making the best.

Your life already follows this pattern. Think of your influence zones:

> Jerusalem—your immediate relationships

> Judea—the next circle of colleagues, neighbors, and friends

> Samaria—people unlike you but within reach

> The ends of the earth—people you'll never meet but who'll be affected by those you've influenced

The compounding effect works like financial compounded interest. Your influence grows when those you've mentored go on to mentor others. You may never see the full return, but it's still accumulating.

> Arrival thinking measures quarterly or annually. Legacy thinking measures generationally.

Turn today's 1440 minutes into momentum.
Download your free tracker at 1440Tracker.com

That requires patience and faith—to invest without controlling the outcome, to plant trees whose shade you'll never sit under.

This perspective also brings freedom. You don't carry the full result. You simply steward the influence you've been given.

And here's the surprising truth: living this way feels lighter, not heavier. It shifts motivation from achievement pressure to gratitude—which has its own chapter coming next.

Take sip of coffee or lemonade and read this slowly:

> Gratitude is the renewable fuel that sustains influence after the applause fades.

Making the Shift Practical

Moving from arrival to legacy isn't a quantum leap; it's a series of small reorientations.

Start by auditing your current commitments through a legacy lens:
Which activities primarily build your platform?
Which ones build others' capacity?
Both matter, but the right balance depends on your season.

Here are three simple experiments for shifting toward legacy right where you are. (

This chapter's Lab will help you with this; feel free to page ahead as you read and capture your notes.)

Identify one person to mentor intentionally for the next six months.

Join or start a small peer-learning group to grow through mutual influence.

Pay attention to your own modeling. Someone's learning how to be a professional, a parent, or a leader just by watching you live.

None of these require big time blocks—just redirected attention. Exhaustion often comes from chasing arrival goals that no longer hold meaning. Legacy, by contrast, energizes because it resonates with purpose.

You don't have to abandon ambition or achievement. You redirect them from accumulation to contribution. Some people may make significant life changes shifting to ROI^2—early retirement to coach, write, or serve. Others will make quiet shifts within their existing roles. Both are valid, and both build legacy.

The question isn't, "How much can I change?"
It's, "What one shift can I make this week toward contribution?"

You've spent quality time learning how to arrive. You're good at it. Now you get to learn how to leave—
   leave a legacy, leave your influence, leave fruit that remains.

That's what Legacy-Level Living is all about.

Case Stories

Miss May Rankin, Professor, and Alfred Lunt

Upon enrolling at Carroll College (now Carroll University) in Waukesha, Wisconsin, Alfred Lunt was soon discovered by Rankin, who recognized his profound talent and potential for the theater. She cast him in every one of her six annual productions, offering him not just roles, but genuine creative challenges and opportunities for growth.

Miss Rankin was an innovator in theater education, developing Carroll's formal theater curriculum in 1901—ahead of its time for an American college. She insisted that her students, including Lunt, embrace all facets of dramatic art: acting, directing, and even designing scenery. Through this process, Lunt learned discipline, leadership, and a deep respect for the craft of theater. Under Rankin's mentorship, he was able to create and perform new material, and by his second year had already worked up his own comedy routines, performing throughout Wisconsin.

Rankin's rigorous standards set the foundation for Lunt's lifelong devotion to the theater, both as an actor and director. Her encouragement did more than hone his technique; it gave him the courage to pursue acting professionally at a time when such a path was far from secure. The confidence she instilled empowered Lunt to seek his future in Boston, paving the way for his extraordinary career on Broadway and beyond.

Alfred Lunt's later achievements—his celebrated partnership with Lynn Fontanne, his status as one of America's greatest actors, and his trailblazing naturalistic performance style—can all be traced back to the foundations laid at Carroll College under May Rankin's tireless tutelage. Through her belief in young talent and mastery of educational theater, Rankin left an indelible mark not only on Lunt, but on American drama itself.

Prof Hendricks, Multiplier

Howard G. Hendricks—affectionately known as "Prof"—was a legendary professor at Dallas Theological Seminary whose life's calling was to "disciple and mentor future leaders through intentional relationships and practical challenge."

Over his sixty years at DTS, he mentored more than 12,000 men and women, shaping pastors, authors, and speakers whose ripple effects are felt globally.

At the heart of Hendricks's approach was a relentless focus on multiplication—training students not only to follow Christ personally, but to actively seek out and mentor others in turn. His mentoring style was highly personal and demanding; for those aspiring to learn under him, he deliberately set early-morning meeting times, often beginning discipleship sessions at dawn. This practice was a filter: Hendricks believed showing up consistently and sacrificially was the first test of genuine commitment, a way of challenging would-be proteges to prioritize spiritual growth over comfort. His mentees recall that these early morning gatherings were not just about knowledge, but about life-on-life modeling of discipline, humility, prayer, and pragmatism.

The influence of Prof Hendricks extended far beyond the classroom. He established the Center for Christian Leadership at DTS, creating programs and small-group communities that multiplied his vision for discipleship across generations of students. Evangelical leaders, including Chuck Swindoll, Tony Evans, David Jeremiah, Robert Jeffress, and Chip Ingram, trace their ministries to Hendricks's mentoring, describing him as more than a teacher—a friend who believed in their potential, challenged their thinking, and supported their growth at every stage.

Hendricks often said that his greatest joy was seeing transformation blossom in those he mentored, when students became disciples themselves, multiplying Christlike influence in churches, communities, and nations. To Prof, the measure of a life well-lived was not just knowledge or accomplishment, but legacy: changed lives who went on to change others.

Howard Hendricks leaves a timeless model for mentoring—one built on challenging expectations, persistent investment, and a passion for seeing every protégé become a generational influencer for Christ.

Shane, and the elementary-school seed that flourished.

Shane and his sister Shaelah were the children of good friends Merlin and June who sang in the church choir I directed in Downers Grove, Illinois. Each week they'd sit in the pews while choir practiced, the last thing on the Wednesday series of events at church.

One week I wanted to play a demo recording for the choir but the sound booth was in the balcony, and the choir was on the platform.
I wonder ...

"Shane, would you be willing to press PLAY for me in a few minutes, help me play this demo for choir?" He was responsible, his dad was an audiophile so I knew he'd respect the equipment up there.

He agreed, grabbed his book and we went to the balcony. I showed him the controls and how to adjust the volume if needed. Things went just right during rehearsal, and I thanked him for his help.

A couple of Sundays later I noticed Shane sitting behind the sound desk during Sunday morning church, watching the audio team at work. "Would you like to learn that system?" I asked, "Once you know your way around, we might be able to schedule you for a Sunday night now and then." He loved the idea so I introduced him to Kevin, a sound tech who actually liked kids. They hit it off, and soon Shane was in demand, even as a student.

We moved away in '93 and I lost track of Shane and his family for a while. Years later we connected on LinkedIn, struck up a conversation and he volunteered that he'd gone on to earn his degree and other credentials, and at that time owned Web Feat Productions, which had a 30-foot audio and visual truck and mobile studio that served Christian conventions and conferences! "When people ask me how I got started," he said, "I smile and tell them 'Well, it all started when my mom and dad's choir director asked me to press PLAY one night to play a demo recording at rehearsal.'" *(near quote)*

Who knew?

LAB: Legacy Audit & Influence Mapping

Thinking Shift:

From: "Achievement proves my worth."

To: "Contribution measures my impact."

Key Insight:
Legacy is built when arrival moments become launchpads for investing in others, not endpoints for personal gain.

ACTION: The Legacy Audit & Influence Experiment

Step 1: Arrival Reflection & Storywork (30 minutes)

- Write about a personal "arrival" moment—a milestone that felt hollow or incomplete after the initial celebration.
- Name what you achieved, but also describe the tension or dissonance you felt.
- Reflect specifically: Who was present? What was said (use dialogue)?
- Ask: Did this moment feel like fulfillment or like a prompt for something greater?

    End with the realization: "I mistook the climb for the purpose.

Step 2: Mapping Your Influence Zones (20 minutes)

- Draw concentric circles to map your zones of influence:
    - Jerusalem: Closest relationships (family, direct reports, close friends)
    - Judea: Next circle of colleagues, professional peers, neighbors
    - Samaria: People different from you but within reach—distant coworkers, online communities, etc.
    - Ends of the Earth: Those influenced indirectly by the people you've already impacted.
- In each zone, list at least two individuals and write what kind of legacy you want to leave with each (mentorship, doors opened, wisdom shared).

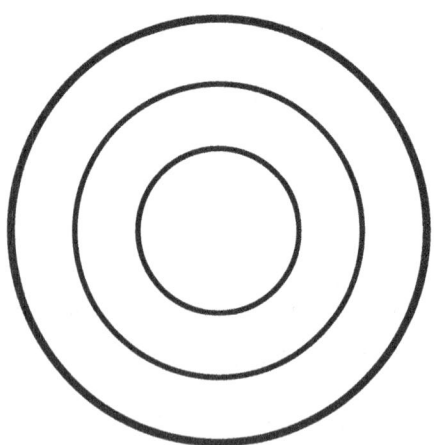

Turn today's 1440 minutes into momentum.
Download your free tracker at 1440Tracker.com

Step 3: Legacy-Level Commitment Plan (Next Month)

- Choose ONE person from any zone to intentionally invest in for four weeks (mentor, support, open a door).

    1 _____

    2 _____

    3 _____

    4 _____

- Journal weekly:
    - What legacy action did you take?
    - How did it feel compared to typical achievement-driven tasks?
    - What signs of multiplied influence appeared?

    1 _____

    2 _____

    3 _____

    4 _____

Checkpoint Milestone:
❏ *You've written a legacy reflection, mapped your influence zones, made a month-long legacy commitment, and tracked impact beyond yourself.*

Scriptural Footings:

On Transformational Gratitude:

- Psalm 103:1-5 – Forget not all benefits
- 1 Thessalonians 5:18 – In all circumstances
- Colossians 3:15-17 – Thankful hearts
- Ephesians 5:20 – Always giving thanks
- Philippians 4:6 – With thanksgiving

On as Worship:

- Psalm 100:1-5 – Enter with thanksgiving
- Psalm 50:23 – Sacrifice of thanksgiving
- Leviticus 7:12 – Thanksgiving offering
- 1 Chronicles 29:13-14 – Everything comes from You
- Hebrews 13:15 – Sacrifice of praise

On Generous Living:

- 2 Corinthians 9:6-11 – Sow generously
- Acts 20:35 – More blessed to give
- Proverbs 11:25 – Generous soul prospers
- Luke 6:38 – Give and receive
- Matthew 10:8 – Freely give

On Stewardship & Abundance:

- Luke 12:48 – Much given, much required
- 1 Peter 4:10 – Serve one another
- Matthew 25:21 – Faithful with little
- Deuteronomy 8:17-18 – Power to gain wealth
- Malachi 3:10 – Test Me in this

Turn today's 1440 minutes into momentum.
Download your free tracker at 1440Tracker.com

On Gratitude's Renewal:

- Psalm 30:11-12 – Mourning to dancing
- Isaiah 61:3 – Garment of praise
- Lamentations 3:22-23 – Mercies are new
- Philippians 4:11-13 – Content in all

Turn today's 1440 minutes into momentum.
Download your free tracker at 1440Tracker.com

CHAPTER 4: Gratitude, The Transformation Engine

I served a church in Delafield, Wisconsin, for 10 years, and in 1996, we began a new initiative in conjunction with my master's thesis at Moody Graduate School: Disciple-making within the worship arts venue.

We studied the scriptural foundations and principles for establishing the disciple-making aspects that should be at work. Musicians, artists and technicians shouldn't have to join a separate discipleship group; they should learn and develop those abilities right where they're serving. One evening near the end of our time together, Bernie, our bassist, a classically trained musician who was also vice president of wealth management at a local bank, said, "You know this flies in the face of how we're trained as classical musicians, right? Don't share a fingering, don't share a bowing, or next season they might be first chair, and you'll be turning their pages! But here it is in the text (meaning the Bible). I say, Let's do this".

One by one, around the table, we all agreed. It wasn't a vote; it was developing consensus about our new vision, and how we would measure success, though we didn't know at that point what it would ultimately look like.

Ten or twelve weeks later, Bernie stopped in at my office on his way home from work and announced in his lighthearted way, "Well, I need to give up half of my gigs, Phil."

As I explored what he meant, I discovered that he had been working with Mandy, a high school junior and the best bassist at her school. He'd helped her buy a fretless bass guitar so it would feel like the double-bass she played in orchestra and jazz band at school. They'd been practicing, and she was ready to play. Disciple maker worshiper number one.

It didn't take her long; Mandy was working with an underclassman who was soon playing bass with the student ministries praise team.

Jon, our drummer (Bernie's son), multiplied his skills first with one high school drummer, then another. A couple of years later, with a high school freshman who had potential.

We went from my being the worship leader, with a designated substitute if I ever got sick or went on vacation, to a department with four worship leaders who understood our collective philosophy of worship. Tom S, who led from piano; Tom H, a college vocal professor who led from guitar; Jon, who led from guitar because he'd trained someone to play the drums. We helped develop two student worship leaders in high school and opened the gates for two women worship leaders.

At the base of this growth and development was a deep sense of gratitude for what God was doing in our lives and the skills He helped us develop so we could give them back to him.

We praise & worship team members understood that we're ushers, leading people into God's presence and stepping aside. Prompters to help God's people offer him their heartfelt praise and adoration. It was a way of giving Him the gifts we'd been given and the skills that we'd been encouraged to develop.

Turn today's 1440 minutes into momentum.
Download your free tracker at 1440Tracker.com

Jesus' instructions to make disciples, coupled with Paul's words to his I, Timothy: "Teach others the things you've learned from me," were both a mandate and a privilege. Ours wasn't the expected don't-share-a-fingering, don't-share-a-bowing; it was a quiet, multiply-&-share generosity. And it was delightfully contagious.

The Mechanics of Genuine Thanks

Gratitude is more than saying thanks. It's a way of seeing. A posture that changes how you read your own story. Some people treat gratitude like a social courtesy—polite, appropriate, but shallow. Others live it like oxygen. That's what we're aiming for. Gratitude that renews, not just reacts.

Gratitude operates on three levels: transactional, relational, and transformational.

Transactional gratitude is surface-level courtesy. "Thanks for helping with that project." Polite, appropriate, safe. It costs nothing.

Relational gratitude goes deeper. "Thank you for believing in me when I doubted myself." That builds connection, deepens relationship, widens trust.

Transformational gratitude sits deeper still. It changes how you understand your story. It helps you see that your journey was not self-made but supported, that the thread of providence runs through every chapter.

Most people stay at the transactional level because it's comfortable. You can say it without revealing much.

Turn today's 1440 minutes into momentum.
Download your free tracker at 1440Tracker.com

Transformational gratitude requires three things: specificity, vulnerability, and recognition.

- **Specificity** means naming exactly what you're thankful for and why it mattered.
- **Vulnerability** means admitting you needed what they gave.
- **Recognition** means realizing your story looks different because of their contribution.

You can hear the difference: "Thanks for the recommendation" versus "Your recommendation opened a door I couldn't open alone. You saw potential I didn't yet see and spent your credibility on my behalf. That changed my trajectory and showed me what advocacy looks like."

The second expression acknowledges dependence. And that's where transformation starts.

Many professionals resist that level of honesty because Dependence feels like weakness. But it's not weakness; it's truth. Nobody builds alone.

> Dependence feels like weakness. But it's not weakness; it's truth. Nobody builds alone.

When you practice specific, vulnerable, recognizing gratitude, several things happen at once. You see your story more accurately. You honor the investment you once took for granted.

Turn today's 1440 minutes into momentum.
Download your free tracker at 1440Tracker.com

You model influence worth replicating. You experience humility that doesn't shrink you but enlarges you. And often, your relationships grow in depth you hadn't thought possible.

In Scripture, gratitude was never vague. The Psalms name God's specific actions, celebrate them publicly, and commit to live differently because of them. Gratitude was a spiritual discipline, not a passing feeling.

Transformational gratitude works the same way. It slows you down. It helps you notice the detail and direction of grace. It turns awareness into worship.

The Renewing Power of Gratitude

Gratitude isn't just backward-looking appreciation;
it's forward-looking renewal.

Research confirms gratitude's measurable effects
—improved sleep, higher resilience, lower stress—
but the deeper work happens in the heart.
Gratitude renews perspective, energy, and generosity.

Here's how:

> It **combats entitlement.** You can't nurse a "I deserve this" attitude while recognizing all you've received.

> It **reframes hardship.** Gratitude reveals what developed in you through difficulty and clarifies how pain shaped purpose.

> It **releases bitterness.** It's hard to stay resentful while rehearsing reasons to be thankful.

It **redirects ambition.** It asks, not "What more can I get?" but "What can I give from what I've received?"

It **restores perspective.** Gratitude zooms out, reminding you the current challenge is part of a larger story still unfolding.

Picture two professionals facing identical setbacks. One fixates on the unfairness, replays wounds, and grows cynical. The other actively practices gratitude—naming teachers, teammates, lessons, and unseen help along the way. Same circumstance. Different energy. The grateful one moves forward lighter, clearer, more generous.

Many high achievers feel tired not because they lack capacity, but because they rehearse what's wrong more than what's right. Gratitude reverses that drain. It's not toxic positivity; it's accurate accounting. Both the problems and the provisions are real. But whichever you dwell on determines your energy.

Like exercise, gratitude's benefits compound through practice. Sporadic bursts help briefly; consistency transforms.
Daily reflection. Weekly journaling. Occasional letters.
Over time, it rewires internal dialogue.

Grateful people hold influence naturally. They give freely because they recognize how freely they've received. They stay grounded during disruption because gratitude keeps perspective in play. They honor others easily because recognition is habit. They stay hopeful because gratitude starves cynicism.

Tired leaders often ask, "Where will I find energy for legacy work?" The answer is gratitude. Obligation drains; gratitude renews. "Should" exhausts. "Grateful to" energizes.

Turn today's 1440 minutes into momentum.
Download your free tracker at 1440Tracker.com

Influence that flows from duty fades;
influence that flows from gratitude grows stronger.

Gratitude as Worship

For people of faith, gratitude is more than wellness practice—it's worship.

Old Testament thanksgiving offerings weren't transactions paying for blessings; they were declarations of recognition: "Everything comes from You, and we give only what comes from Your hand."

Psalms of thanksgiving follow a pattern—specific recollection, public declaration, renewed commitment.

That pattern still works. When you thank someone, you recall specifics ("you did this"), you make it visible ("I want others to know what you did"), and you express intent to steward it ("I'll carry this forward in how I live").

This posture reframes influence itself. You're not creating a personal brand of legacy; you're stewarding divine gifts received through human hands. The pressure to prove something decreases; the sense of purpose increases.

That's the doxological life—a life shaped by gratitude, recognition, and giving. It says not, "Look what I've built," but "Look what I've been given and what I'm doing with it."

Such a life keeps ego in check, keeps joy alive, sustains generosity, and creates worship in action. Influence itself becomes offering.

- Mentoring a younger colleague becomes thanksgiving for mentors who guided you.
- Opening doors becomes gratitude for doors opened once for you.

Turn today's 1440 minutes into momentum.
Download your free tracker at 1440Tracker.com

- Modeling character becomes gratitude for character you once witnessed.

Every act of influence becomes thank-you language in motion. You're not giving out of guilt but out of overflow. Not "I must influence" but "I get to influence—it's how I say Thank You."

From Private Feeling to Public Practice

Gratitude that stays inside remains incomplete. It warms the heart but doesn't transform the world unless expressed.

Transformation speeds up through expression. Gratitude takes tangible form three ways:

> **Direct** —you tell the person specifically what you appreciate and why.
> **Indirect** —you tell others about that person's investment in your life.
> **Enacted** —you live in ways that steward what they gave you, multiplying its reach.

Expression makes gratitude real. Thinking grateful thoughts stays abstract. Putting them into words makes them concrete.

Writing and delivering a letter of thanks sharpens memory, deepens relationships, and lifts both giver and receiver.

Here's a challenge: thank three people this month.
One easy—someone you see often.
One harder—someone you haven't spoken to in years.
And one symbolic—someone gone or out of reach. Write them anyway.

The act of writing clarifies memory and fuels commitment to steward what you received.

Turn today's 1440 minutes into momentum.
Download your free tracker at 1440Tracker.com

It's normal for this to feel awkward at first. Gratitude requires vulnerability. Even if they "already know," hearing it matters—to them, and even more to you. Clarity grows in the act of expression.

Expressed gratitude becomes embodied gratitude. It shifts inner awareness outward into relational action.

This is the pivot point of your journey.

> Recognize (Chapters 1–3),
> Reframe (this chapter),
> Renew through gratitude (next chapter), then
> Redirect toward generosity.

Gratitude connects foundation to flow. Without gratitude, influence feels forced. With it, influence becomes natural overflow.

The Gratitude–Influence Cycle

Here's the rhythm:

Gratitude leads to generosity.
　Generosity creates influence.
　　Influence multiplies gratitude again.

You recognize what you've received—that fills your tank.
　From fullness, you give.
　　That generosity shapes others, prompting their gratitude.
　　　The cycle continues.

This is how influence multiplies. Through grateful stewardship, not striving.

If you're feeling empty, start here. Gratitude fills the reservoir. Influence flows from overflow, not depletion.

Arrival thinking says, "I must produce more." Legacy thinking says, "I've received much; how do I steward it?"

Turn today's 1440 minutes into momentum.
Download your free tracker at 1440Tracker.com

One drains. The other renews.

When in doubt, pause and take inventory. I'm not talking about fluffy positive thinking. I'm talking about accurate remembering. List the names, moments, and mercies that shaped you. That list is your energy source, and that source never runs dry.

Transition to Engaging Gratitude: Awareness to Action

Gratitude doesn't just change how you *see* your story; it changes how you *live* it. You're about to pivot from feeling grateful to living gratefully.

The movement from "I'm grateful for what I received" to "I'll steward what I received by giving to others," starts here.

This isn't repayment. It isn't obligation. It's overflow. Generosity that flows from guilt depletes;
generosity that flows from gratitude renews.

Read those lines again.

You'll pass through four stages in the gratitude journey:

- Stage 1: **Unconscious ingratitude**
  Taking gifts for granted.
- Stage 2: **Conscious gratitude**
  Recognizing what you've received.

- Stage 3: **Expressed gratitude**
  Communicating thanks clearly and specifically.
- Stage 4: **Enacted gratitude**
  Stewarding what you've received by investing in others.

Internal gratitude that stays private can become self-focused:
(to others) "Look how blessed I am."

External gratitude becomes others-focused:
(to yourself) "Look what I can give from what I've been given."

The biblical pattern has always been "blessed to be a blessing". (Genesis 12:2).

> You're not a reservoir; you're a conduit. Influence flows through you, not to you.

That shift can feel difficult at times because the professional world rewards the accumulation of knowledge, capital, and reputation.
Legacy redirects toward circulation through people, opportunities, and systems.

Your resources, abilities, and networks aren't possessions to protect; they're stewardships to deploy.
We guard possessions. Stewardships stay active.

This is your Gratitude Shift—where awareness turns to action, and grace received becomes grace extended.

It can be a little scary at first pass, because most people don't think like this. Some, not understanding, may even criticize you.

Turn today's 1440 minutes into momentum.
Download your free tracker at 1440Tracker.com

The Mechanics of Generous Living

Generosity isn't only about money. It's a posture. A way of holding what you have.

Generous people give from many currencies:

- ❖ time,
- ❖ attention,
- ❖ wisdom,
- ❖ connections,
- ❖ opportunity,
- ❖ encouragement,
- ❖ resources.

> The abundance mindset says there's enough to share. The scarcity mindset fears running out and tightens its grip. The mindset you live from determines how much influence you can carry.

Relational Generosity

Giving attention, presence, then presence again. In a distracted age, attention is rare currency. Fully showing up with eye contact, slow listening, and unhurried conversation, transfers more influence than any platform can.

If you arrive but don't attend (think undivided-attention), your presence loses power. Generous presence requires more *you* in the moments you already have. When it comes to relationships,

Turn today's 1440 minutes into momentum.
Download your free tracker at 1440Tracker.com

quality comes wrapped in quantity.

Wisdom Generosity

You've accumulated stories. Scars. Insights. Much of your best wisdom came through setbacks. That wisdom has value if you share it. If you give it away.

Tell the stories. Share what failed, not just what worked. It gives others permission to learn without disguising missteps. Competitive professionals tend to hoard wisdom, while legacy professionals multiply it. Writing, mentoring, and teaching are all acts of wisdom generosity.

Resource Generosity

Resource Generosity includes connections, introductions, access, and, yes, finances. Your current influence likely opens doors others can't yet reach. Pause for a moment to consider that opening those doors may change someone's life the way someone once changed yours!

Financial giving matters, but an even greater leverage often comes from relational capital; an introduction, a recommendation, an opportunity.

Across all three spheres runs one truth:
Generosity from gratitude is sustainable.
Giving from duty depletes; giving from abundance renews.
Gratitude opens the fuel line.

God's Design for Generosity

Generosity sits at the center of God's design for flourishing.

The Sowing Principle (2 Corinthians 9:6–11)

Whoever sows generously reaps generously. I encourage you to pause, look up and read the verses above in your favorite translation.

This isn't "give to get." It's "give because you've received." Paul's point was shared impact, not personal prosperity. Generosity fuels ministry, which fuels transformation, which fuels more generosity!

Your influence works the same way. The harvest may not return directly to you, but it will certainly multiply through others.

The Faithful Steward Principle (Matthew 25:14–30)

Three servants received resources. Two invested. One hid his. The fearful one, protecting rather than multiplying, got it wrong.

The same applies to influence. It's tempting to guard our wisdom or protect our opportunities. But stewardship means investing what was entrusted to you, even without guarantees. It's easy to get snagged on that. Some investments multiply; some don't. Faithful stewards keep giving anyway.

The Faith That Works Principle (James 2:15–16)

If you see need but do nothing, what good is that?
Faith without works is dead.

Turn today's 1440 minutes into momentum.
Download your free tracker at 1440Tracker.com

Gratitude that doesn't produce generosity has the same problem. It's incomplete. Gratitude without generosity is dead. (Ouch!)

Don't close the book, keep reading. Let's unwrap this.

> True faith and true gratitude both overflow.

Gratitude received without generosity expressed misses the finish line. Generosity is both worship and witness. When you invest in others, open doors, or share wisdom, you're not performing some virtue, you're reflecting God's character.

> Monday's generosity is Sunday's worship in action.

The Generosity/Influence Connection

When you're generous with wisdom, time, or opportunity, people sense your motives. You're invested in their good, not your gain. That trust opens influence faster than charisma ever could.

People resist manipulation but lean toward genuine investment. They know the difference intuitively.

Turn today's 1440 minutes into momentum.
Download your free tracker at 1440Tracker.com

Leaders who chase influence through image get followers for a time, but leaders who build influence through generosity gain partners for a lifetime.

Legacy-level leaders find their influence amplified because their generosity communicates safety. People want to live & grow near people who don't use them as stepping-stones.

You hold influence today that you didn't have years ago. Experience, resources, credibility, and voice.
Will you hoard it?
Or release it?

The generous posture multiplies joy,
      multiplies trust,
         and multiplies impact.

Influence grows in circulation. It always has.

Making the Shift Practical

Gratitude that moves toward generosity takes practice, but pressure is counter-productive.

Try these three activities to help your gratitude grow & develop. Think "cultivate" or "nurture".

The Weekly Gift: Each **week**, choose one person and give one of four meaningful things. Time, encouragement, introduction, or small resource. Make it specific (not generic). Watch what happens inside you as generosity becomes a rhythm instead of a recurring to-do item.

The Mentoring Investment: Pick one person this **quarter** to mentor intentionally. You don't need to tell them ahead of time, that might actually frighten them. You can formalize it later if you want to but meet regularly. "When's your coffee break? I'll join you." Share honestly. Create learning goals together. One committed relationship outweighs three casual ones.

The Abundance Audit: Each **month**, review your resources—time, skills, access. I recommend the last Sunday evening of the month in a quiet, relaxed setting. Where are you hoarding? Where could you open your hand? What might happen if you shared more freely?

All three of these practices keep life simple but purposeful.
This isn't adding a burden; you're redirecting capacity you already have. The power source is gratitude and the output is generosity.

Do you feel like you're coming up over the crest of a hill about now?
You should, you've recognized influence received.
You've reframed success through legacy.
You're learning gratitude's renewing rhythm and
you're ready for generosity—It's compound legacy's next step.

Case Stories

Siblings are worthy of our love, time and intentional investment. They don't have to be enemies or even competitors; with careful intentionality, siblings can be lifetime collaborators and mutual investors. My sisters and I are "Exhibit A".

Once Stu Booth turned my perspective right side up that week at camp, I began to see my sisters as allies, rather than resident annoyances and targets for my mischief. They began to look up to me as every big brother dreams — or should — and I came to respect them. We became friends and fellow musicians, our violin, trombone, and piano trios occasionally featured at church. We cheered each other on. Encouraged each other.

Vonnie became my preferred accompanist, and I asked her —a college freshman— to accompany me for my Senior Recital. She points back to what she learned from me, becoming an excellent accompanist, and today entrusts those skills to her piano students. Both Vonnie and Jo play and accompany regularly in their churches.

Jo and her husband, Rick, have for years quietly invested in people who have hesitant or unspoken needs, coming alongside, investing tangible and intangible help. Currently they're vested in our mom's well-being, hosting and caring for her late in life, keeping us well-informed across the miles.

Vonnie and her pastor husband, Rob, apparently see the potential in our continuing to learn from each other; they were the first two to join The Vibrance Community as Pathfinders in late 2024.

Turn today's 1440 minutes into momentum.
Download your free tracker at 1440Tracker.com

Deeply grateful for each other, the three of us share organizational tips, ministry resources, and tips & smiles on social media. We're quick to celebrate each other's success and encourage one another.

LAB: The Gratitude Transformation Practice

Thinking Shift:

From: "Gratitude is a nice feeling I should have often."

To: "Gratitude is a transformative force that changes how I see my story and live my life."

Key Insight: Gratitude that stays internal is incomplete. When gratitude moves from awareness to expression to action, it becomes the engine that powers sustainable, generous influence.

ACTION: The Transformational Gratitude Cycle

Step 1: The Transformational Gratitude Practice (30 minutes)

Write three transformational gratitude letters using this structure:

Letter 1 - Recent Gratitude: Someone from the last 5 years
___

Letter 2 - Distant Gratitude: Someone from 10+ years ago
___

Letter 3 - Difficult Gratitude: Someone whose influence came through challenge
___

For each letter, include:

Specificity: "You did this specific thing..."

Vulnerability: "It mattered because I needed..."

Recognition: "It changed my story by..."

Turn today's 1440 minutes into momentum.
Download your free tracker at 1440Tracker.com

Deliver at least one letter this week
(mail, email, or in person).

Step 2: The Abundance Audit (20 minutes)

Inventory what you've received that you can now give:

• Relational Capital: Attention, presence, time—
who needs yours?

_____
_____

• Wisdom Capital: Experience, knowledge, insight—
who could benefit?

_____
_____

• Resource Capital: Access, opportunities, connections—
who are you positioned to help?

_____
_____

For each category, identify 2-3 specific assets you have to give.

• Relational Capital:

_____
_____

• Wisdom Capital:

_____
_____

• Resource Capital:

_____
_____

Turn today's 1440 minutes into momentum.
Download your free tracker at 1440Tracker.com

Step 3: The Weekly Generosity Experiment (Next 4 weeks)

Commit to giving something meaningful each week:

• Week 1: Give relational generosity (sustained attention to one person)
_____
_____

• Week 2: Give wisdom generosity (share hard-won insight with someone navigating similar challenge)
_____
_____

• Week 3: Give resource generosity (make an introduction or create an opportunity)
_____
_____

• Week 4: Give sacrificially (something that costs you—time, reputation, convenience)
_____
_____

Journal after each: How did giving from gratitude feel different than giving from obligation?

Checkpoint Milestone:
❏ *I've written and delivered at least one transformational gratitude letter, and I've practiced four weeks of intentional generosity flowing from gratitude rather than guilt.*

Scriptural Footings

On Transformational Gratitude:
- Psalm 103:1-5 – Forget not all benefits
- 1 Thessalonians 5:18 – In all circumstances
- Colossians 3:15-17 – Thankful hearts
- Ephesians 5:20 – Always giving thanks
- Philippians 4:6 – With thanksgiving

On Gratitude as Worship:
- Psalm 100:1-5 – Enter with thanksgiving
- Psalm 50:23 – Sacrifice of thanksgiving
- Leviticus 7:12 – Thanksgiving offering
- 1 Chronicles 29:13-14 – Everything comes from You
- Hebrews 13:15 – Sacrifice of praise

On Generous Living:
- 2 Corinthians 9:6-11 – Sow generously
- Acts 20:35 – More blessed to give
- Proverbs 11:25 – Generous soul prospers
- Luke 6:38 – Give and receive
- Matthew 10:8 – Freely give

On Stewardship & Abundance:
- Luke 12:48 – Much given, much required
- 1 Peter 4:10 – Serve one another
- Matthew 25:21 – Faithful with little
- Deuteronomy 8:17-18 – Power to gain wealth
- Malachi 3:10 – Test Me in this

Turn today's 1440 minutes into momentum.
Download your free tracker at 1440Tracker.com

On Gratitude's Renewal:

- Psalm 30:11-12 – Mourning to dancing
- Isaiah 61:3 – Garment of praise
- Lamentations 3:22-23 – Mercies are new
- Philippians 4:11-13 – Content in all

CHAPTER 5: Return on Invested Influence

Doug, Ruth, and their girls were part of the church I mentioned in the last chapter. We served together for 10 years. Doug and Ruth sang in the choir and were part of the small group that met in our home. Later, they hosted a group in their own home.

In revisiting those years recently, I discovered quite to my surprise, that Doug learned more from our choir rehearsals than I had intended. I taught more than I drilled in choir practice, and his skills and confidence grew as a result. So much so that when their pharmacy and gift shop acquired a new building, he included a hidden stage. Doug would frequently solo at special events, singing Elvis Presley songs. "Wouldn't have had the confidence were it not for choir," he smiled.

Ruth learned in our years together the value of studying the Word and books based on the Word, side by side. In choir, her confidence and skills became strong enough she felt comfortable saying Yes to an invitation to lead the children's church praise & worship, and she thrived there.

They established in choir that our focus always belongs on our Savior, whom we serve with our best available skills. It's never to be a performance for our own glory or aggrandizement.

A surprise surfaced at the end of the conversation when Ruth, with a smile, told about when Becky, their oldest daughter, then a high school student, was part of a girls quartet I formed to sing Amy Grant's "Breath of Heaven" one Christmas. It was so well-received, I asked them to sing it again next year, which they did. I'd frequently invite Becky to sing when I learned she'd be home from college on vacation. Her mom said that being sought out that way boosted her confidence at a crucial time. And it stuck. No, it grew. Becky currently sings the national anthem for the honor flights out of Milwaukee, Wisconsin.

Sometimes it's years before you learn the full effects of your investment in people. You can't check in on them like you do your 401(k), you just hear — or see — and your heart swells up - with gratitude. "I'm glad I invested."

The metrics that matter for legacy are different from metrics that matter for arrival. Recognizing those differences changes how you invest in others.

Redefining ROI

Traditional ROI has served us well. It measures gain relative to cost, helping leaders make smart choices about money, time, and effort. Financial ROI isn't a bad scorecard—it's necessary for responsible management. Companies run on it. Households track it. Donors expect it.

But financial ROI can only measure part of what really matters. It tells you whether an investment paid off in dollars and cents, not whether it created lasting value. For Legacy-Level Living, the question shifts from "What return am I getting?" to "What return are others getting through me?"

That's the essence of ROI^2—Return on Invested Influence. It redefines success by measuring others' growth, not your accumulation. It's not about financial yield. It's about human

Turn today's 1440 minutes into momentum.
Download your free tracker at 1440Tracker.com

yield—capacity multiplied through your presence, wisdom, and generosity.

Three questions form the core of ROI^2.

Who developed because of your investment?

"Who did you help?" Helping implies hierarchy. <u>Developing</u> implies partnership. Growth together. You learn while they grow.

Think about what's changed in those you've influenced. Did they gain skills, confidence, or courage? Did they step through a door you helped open? Did they become more capable because of time you gave or insight you shared?

Ask the deeper mentor question: if you disappeared tomorrow, who would be less equipped because you're no longer here? That's your influence footprint—not measured in square footage or financial statements, but in people who stand taller because you invested in them.

What did you build that will outlast you?

Temporary success fades with memory. Enduring impact continues through systems, structures, and cultures you create.

Maybe you built a cohesive team that now functions smoothly without you. Maybe you documented processes that prevent future mistakes. Maybe you mentored leaders who now lead others with integrity.

These aren't monuments with your name on them; they're frameworks others will climb on long after you're gone. The preparation-maker question works here: what are you building for people who don't yet know your name?

Turn today's 1440 minutes into momentum.
Download your free tracker at 1440Tracker.com

Legacy thinkers play the long game. They measure success in decades, not quarters.

Whose potential did you unlock?

Everyone carries dormant talent waiting for recognition. Sometimes the spark is encouragement; sometimes opportunity. Either way, influence happens when you notice what others overlook.

The Barnabas questions fit perfectly: who have you championed when others ignored them? Whose voice did you amplify? Whose door did you help open?

Invisible investment counts too. The person who blossomed because you quietly believed in them. The employee who stayed because you saw their worth when they didn't. Legacy grows in those invisible moments.

These three questions form the ROI^2 framework—an assessment tool that measures contribution, not collection.

Traditional success asks, "What did I achieve? What title did I earn? What income did I reach?"

Legacy success asks, "Who grew? What systems last? Whose future did I influence?"

Both matter. But for those who have already achieved enough, ROI^2 provides the metrics that finally satisfy.

We know this instinctively. Research confirms it. End-of-life reflections rarely circle back to earnings or accolades. They focus on impact, meaning, and relationships. Why wait until the end to measure what matters? Shift the metrics now.

Turn today's 1440 minutes into momentum.
Download your free tracker at 1440Tracker.com

Success Through Faithful Use

The parable of the talents in Matthew 25 comes alive when read through contribution, not accumulation. The master gives resources, then steps away. Two servants invest and multiply what they've received. One buries his talent because he's afraid.

Most interpretations emphasize productivity. But look closer.

> The faithful servants weren't praised for personal gain. They were commended for wise stewardship—accepting what wasn't theirs and multiplying it for the good of another.

That's the heart of ROI². Faithful use means taking the wisdom, experience, and access entrusted to you and investing them to increase others' capacity.

Did you notice? The third servant's failure wasn't technical, it was relational. He misunderstood trust. Instead of investing, he protected. Fear ruled him.

You've accumulated wisdom and credibility through decades of work. The question now isn't "How will I protect this?" but "How will I use this to multiply others?"

Faithful stewardship always includes risk. You'll mentor people who waste the opportunity. Open doors some walk past. Offer insights someone ignores. That's part of the process. You're responsible for investment, not outcome.

Turn today's 1440 minutes into momentum.
Download your free tracker at 1440Tracker.com

Some investments fail—but others flourish beyond your imagination. If you invest in ten people and three flourish, your influence has multiplied thirtyfold. The faithful servants in the story didn't retire with their success; they were invited into greater responsibility: "You've been faithful with little; I'll entrust you with more."

Legacy-level stewardship works the same way.

Faithful use expands capacity—not in control, but in contribution.

Contribution Over Extraction

Every relationship carries tension between extraction and contribution.

The extraction mindset thinks, "What can I get from this?" The contribution mindset asks, "What can I give here?"

Extraction evaluates people by utility. It networks for advantage. It shows up when benefit is clear. The marketplace rewards that posture—it optimizes efficiency and strategy. But relationally, it drains both giver and receiver. Extraction leaves residue: people feel used, not valued.

Contribution does the opposite. It seeks places to invest, connect, and serve. It gives attention without agenda. Contribution multiplies trust. And trust grows influence.

When people sense you're contributing to their development, not using them for yours, they respond with openness. Influence deepens beyond compliance—it becomes partnership.

Audit your own relationships through this lens. Some will be mutual—peer exchanges where both give and receive. Some will be extractive out of necessity, like hiring consultants or paying for expertise. That's fine. The question is posture.

Is extraction your norm or your exception?

If your default posture is contribution, you'll find renewed joy and increased influence. The paradox is simple: giving energizes more than taking because contribution aligns with how you were designed.

The most generous professionals are rarely the most exhausted. They draw from abundance, not scarcity. Extraction fights your design.

Contribution fulfills it.

The Multiplication Effect

Contribution thinking changes math. Addition says, "I accomplished this." Multiplication says, "Someone else accomplished more because I invested."

Jesus could have personally addressed crowds every day. Instead, he poured deeply into twelve and released them to reach thousands. The pattern is timeless—focus deeply to multiply widely.

If you personally influence a hundred people, that's addition. If you deeply develop ten who each influence ten—and those ten influence ten more—that's a thousand. The exponential curve begins with patient development.

Multiplication takes faith because you won't see all its results. But that's what legacy is: influence measured in generations, not quarters.

Turn today's 1440 minutes into momentum.
Download your free tracker at 1440Tracker.com

Consider the implications in your world:

- In business, developing leaders who develop leaders.
- In family, modeling faith and character your children will echo to their children.
- In community, equipping others to serve rather than doing all the serving yourself.
- In knowledge work, teaching others to think well rather than merely sharing what you know.

> Your success multiplies when their fruit grows. That's ROI^2—return measured through others' outcomes.

You plant.

They harvest.

And through them, the harvest continues.

Living Contribution Daily

Reframing success as contribution happens day by day.

Morning question: "Who can I contribute to today?"

Evening question: "Whose capacity increased because I showed up?"

Turn today's 1440 minutes into momentum.
Download your free tracker at 1440Tracker.com

Weekly review: "Who developed because of my presence this week?"

Monthly check: "What did I build that will outlast me?"

These new metrics don't replace achievement—they enrich it. Over time, they shift how you define success entirely.
Contribution becomes habit.
And fulfillment grows where anxiety once lived.

The Integration Imperative

All meaningful influence depends on integration—faith, values, and vocation woven together.

Too many professionals live compartmentalized lives: faith for Sunday, performance for Monday. It's not hypocrisy—it's habit. But the split drains energy and weakens influence. You can't live divided and lead effectively.

Integration doesn't mean preaching at work. It means leading with one set of values everywhere. **Integrity** under pressure. **Generosity** in competition. **Stewardship** instead of ownership. **Grace** in conflict.

Faithful integration produces recognizable consistency. People know what to expect from you. They trust the alignment between what you say and who you are.

Unintegrated lives whisper mixed messages. Integrated lives speak clearly without words. Integration isn't about perfection—it's about progress and wholeness. Daily calibration. Honest reflection.

Consistent alignment.

Turn today's 1440 minutes into momentum.
Download your free tracker at 1440Tracker.com

Legacy-level influence grows strongest here—where what you believe and how you behave finally match.

Leading Through Integrity

Integrity comes from the same root as integer—whole, undivided. People of integrity are the same everywhere. They don't adjust values to fit the moment.

Integrity leadership tells truth with grace. It keeps commitments. It owns mistakes. It shares credit freely and advances others' success without fear.

It takes courage to lead this way. Short-term, it might cost you. Long-term, it compounds trust—the rarest currency in leadership. And trust is influence.

You've seen both kinds of leaders: the ambitious compromisers and the consistent builders. Who shaped you more?

Legacy-Level Living invites you to choose: compromise for applause or consistency for impact. Only one leaves lasting influence.

Faith in Everyday Decisions

Integration shows up in small decisions.

How you treat servers, interns, and people with no advantage to offer. How you handle criticism. How you guard confidences. How you spend time and money.

Each choice quietly communicates your true beliefs. People read your daily options more than your spoken convictions.
Your lived faith is your influence.

This isn't legalism—it's calibration. When actions drift away from values, realign. When they match, celebrate progress. Influence grows as integrity deepens.

The Influence Impact

Influence has more power when it's consistent, generous, and integrated. People aren't shaped by your declarations but by your demonstration.

Faith without action is invisible.

Faith lived out loud becomes contagious.

Legacy-Level Living doesn't demand bigger stages. It requires truer stewardship. ROI^2—Return on Invested Influence—is the scorecard worth keeping. It measures what truly endures: people developed, systems sustained, character reproduced, faith lived with integrity.

The same question echoes through every context: Who will flourish because you were here?

That's legacy. That's ROI^2.
And that's a return worth investing your life in.

Case Stories

Mr. Neime - Teacher, and Charles Swindoll

As a shy, stuttering freshman who felt invisible and doubted his own worth, Swindoll was stunned when Mr. Nieme approached him at his locker and said, "Chuck, I want you on my debate team." This simple invitation, coming from a teacher who saw potential in him despite his insecurities, marked the beginning of Swindoll's transformation into a confident communicator and leader.

Swindoll has often recounted how, as a young man, he struggled with a severe stutter and felt like a "shadow boy" in his family and school. He was used to being overlooked and often tried to remain invisible. When Mr. Nieme extended the invitation, Swindoll was incredulous—his immediate reaction was, "Who, m-m-me?" He could not believe that someone would see value in him, especially for a role that required public speaking. Yet, Mr. Nieme's belief in Swindoll's potential was unwavering. This act of encouragement planted a seed of confidence that would grow over time.

Accepting the invitation to join the debate team forced Swindoll to confront his fears head-on. He had to practice speaking and learn to articulate his thoughts clearly. The experience was transformative. Through hard work and the support of his teacher, Swindoll gradually developed his communication skills and self-assurance. This growth did not happen overnight, but the consistent encouragement and high expectations from Mr. Nieme provided the motivation Swindoll needed to persevere.

Swindoll has often credited this experience as foundational to his later success as a pastor, author, and communicator. One person's belief in another can have a profound and lasting impact. Swindoll's story is a testament to the power of encouragement and the importance of seeing potential in others, even when they cannot see it in themselves.

This moment with Mr. Nieme not only changed Charles Swindoll's trajectory but also shaped his philosophy of leadership and mentorship. Sometimes, all it takes is one person to believe in you to unlock your potential and set you on a path of growth and influence.

Mrs. Benz's bold confidence in her husband's invention

Bertha Benz's demonstrative confidence in her husband and his invention in 1888 proved that Karl Benz's Patent Motorwagen was a viable vehicle; her visionary resolve and bold promotion also effectively launched the modern automobile age. Karl Benz, a brilliant engineer and Bertha's husband, had created the first actual automobile. But he was a cautious, reserved businessman, which made it difficult to demonstrate how useful the Motorwagen was beyond short test drives near his workshop.

Bertha, recognizing the world-changing importance of their invention and aware that public skepticism was holding it back, resolved to prove its reliability herself.

On August 5, 1888, before sunrise and without asking Karl's permission, she departed from Mannheim with her teenage sons Eugen and Richard, steering the Model III Motorwagen towards her mother's home in Pforzheim, over 100 kilometers away. This was the first long-distance automobile journey in history, and

Bertha set out in secret because she knew technological and societal doubts needed a dramatic refutation.

The journey was anything but easy. The Motorwagen, primitive by today's standards, broke down several times. Bertha made ad hoc repairs along the way, including clearing a fuel line with her hairpin and sourcing ligroin fuel from a local pharmacy, thus founding the world's first 'gas station'. At one point when the wooden brakes began to fail, she asked a village cobbler to fit them with leather pads—effectively inventing the brake lining and demonstrating practical problem-solving that improved the car's design for all future owners. On steep hill climbs, her sons had to help push the vehicle, inspiring her later suggestion that Benz add a new gear for climbing, further shaping automotive engineering.

Bertha's journey traversed open countryside, small villages, and curious onlookers, each of whom became witness to the viability of Karl's invention and word quickly spread. News of her success and her practical feedback, attracted both local and national press, catalyzing the first surge of public interest and inventories for the new Motorwagen. Even Karl, who awoke to find his creation missing, was astonished and delighted by the publicity and affirmation Bertha's initiative produced.

Through her courage, ingenuity, and business sense, Bertha Benz was far more than her husband's supporter—she was investor, field tester, engineer, and the world's first automotive publicist. Her legendary road trip launched the era of personal transportation, and the company that would later become Mercedes-Benz. Without Bertha Benz's boldness, technical insight, and confidence in her husband's invention, the story of the automobile would have begun very differently.

Turn today's 1440 minutes into momentum.
Download your free tracker at 1440Tracker.com

R.G. LeTeourneau's partnership with God

R.G. LeTourneau's journey of generosity began not from abundance, as one might expect, but during hardship. At age thirty, deeply in debt and unsure of his future, he resolved to make God his literal business partner, a commitment encouraged by his missionary sister's challenge to serve God with his talents. Not just in the church, she urged, but through his work as an inventor and entrepreneur. He began by tithing 10% of his income even though money was scarce, believing that every resource was entrusted to him for a larger purpose.

As his earthmoving equipment business flourished, LeTourneau steadily increased his giving. First 20%. Then 30%. He eventually instituted "reverse tithing," giving away 90% of his personal and company profits while living on just 10%.

This shift didn't happen overnight; it grew out of trusting God with each step, convinced that both generosity and invention are acts of worship.

His greatest joy in this journey was twofold:

First, he loved seeing how his giving could multiply ministry and opportunity: his generosity funded Bible translations, world missions, Christian universities, youth camps, and church plants across continents.

Second, he discovered that the more he gave, the more creative and innovative he became in business—an unexpected effect he described with delight: "I shovel it out, and God shovels it back—but God has a bigger shovel."

Turn today's 1440 minutes into momentum.
Download your free tracker at 1440Tracker.com

For LeTourneau, giving wasn't about sacrifice but about partnership with God, living proof that loosening his grip on wealth opened new doors for service, influence, and joy.

R.G. LeTourneau's story remains a powerful example of abundant living through generous giving. Faith-driven stewardship can transform both industry and lives when one's greatest satisfaction is found in what can be shared.

LAB: Integration & ROI² Assessment

Thinking Shift

From: "Success means what I achieve; faith is what I believe on Sunday."

To: "Success means who develops through me; faith shapes how I work every day."

Key Insight: Legacy-Level Living requires integration—your faith and work aren't separate domains but unified expressions of who you are. ROI² (Return on Invested Influence) measures success by others' development, not your accumulation.

ACTION: The Integration & Investment Audit

Step 1: Measure Your Current ROI² (30 minutes)

Answer the three core questions with specific names and examples:

Question 1: Who developed because of your investment?

- List 5-10 people who grew through relationship with you
- For each: What specifically did they gain? (skills, confidence, opportunities, character)
- Evidence: What can they do now that they couldn't before you invested?

Person	
Gain	Evidence

Question 2: What did you build that outlasts you?

• Organizational cultures, systems, teams, processes, documented knowledge

• For each: Who benefits from it now? Who will benefit in 10 years?

_____
_____
_____
_____
_____
_____
_____
_____

Question 3: Whose potential did you unlock?

• Who did you champion when others overlooked them?

• What doors did you open? What introductions did you make?

• Where are they now as a result?

_____
_____
_____
_____
_____
_____
_____
_____

Your ROI² Score: Rate yourself honestly (1-10)

1 • Accumulating: my returns   Investing: others' returns • 10

1	2	3	4	5	6	7	8	9	10

Turn today's 1440 minutes into momentum.
Download your free tracker at 1440Tracker.com

Step 2: The Integration Assessment (20 minutes)

Evaluate faith-work integration across five domains:

Character Consistency:

• Am I the same person at work, at home, at church? Where do I fragment?

_____
_____

Values Alignment:

• Do my business decisions reflect my faith convictions? Where's the gap?

_____
_____

Service Orientation:

• Do I view my work as calling or career? How does that show?

_____
_____

Stewardship Mindset:

• Do I operate as owner or steward of resources, influence, opportunities?

_____
_____

Witness Through Work:

• Does my marketplace presence demonstrate my faith? How?

_____
_____

Turn today's 1440 minutes into momentum.
Download your free tracker at 1440Tracker.com

For each domain, identify one specific area of misalignment.

Step 3: One Integration Practice + One Investment (Next 90 days)

Integration Practice - Choose One:

❏ Weekly Audit:
  Weekly review of upcoming decisions through faith lens

❏ Evening Examination:
  Daily reflection on where faith shaped work

❏ Accountability Relationship:
  Monthly peer check-in on integration challenges

Investment Action - Choose One:

❏ The Mentoring Commitment:
  Invest deliberately in one person this quarter

❏ The System-Builder:
  Create/document one thing that will outlast you

❏ The Door-Opener:
  Advocate for or introduce one person whose potential you see

Checkpoint Milestone:
❏ *I can articulate my current ROI^2 with specific examples, I've identified where my faith and work are misaligned, and I'm implementing one integration practice and one investment action over the next 90 days.*

Scriptural Footings

On ROI² (Return on Invested Influence):

- Matthew 25:14-30 – Parable of talents
- Luke 19:11-27 – Parable of minas
- 2 Timothy 2:2 – Entrust to faithful
- John 15:16 – Fruit that remains
- Galatians 6:7-9 – Reap what you sow

On Faith-Work Integration:

- Colossians 3:23-24 – Work for the Lord
- 1 Corinthians 10:31 – All for God's glory
- Ephesians 6:5-8 – Serve wholeheartedly
- Titus 2:9-10 – Adorn the doctrine
- 1 Thessalonians 4:11-12 – Work with your hands

On Character & Integrity:

- Proverbs 10:9 – Walk in integrity
- Proverbs 11:3 – Integrity guides
- Psalm 15:1-5 – Who may dwell
- Daniel 6:4-5 – No corruption found
- 2 Corinthians 8:21 – Honorable in all

On Faithful Stewardship:

- 1 Corinthians 4:2 – Faithfulness required
- Luke 16:10-12 – Faithful in little
- 1 Peter 4:10 – Faithful stewards
- Matthew 24:45-46 – Faithful and wise
- Proverbs 3:9-10 – Honor the Lord

On Servant Leadership:

- Mark 10:42-45 – Not to be served
- John 13:12-17 – Wash one another's feet
- Philippians 2:3-8 – Consider others better
- 1 Peter 5:2-3 – Shepherd God's flock

On Multiplication & Discipleship:

- Matthew 28:18-20 – Make disciples
- Acts 1:8 – Concentric circles
- 2 Timothy 2:2 – Teach to teach
- Hebrews 5:12 – Teach others

CHAPTER 6: The Power of Strategic Advocacy

Carol Burnett's remarkable career in comedy and television was launched by a singular act of advocacy—a mysterious, intentional introduction and connection that set her on the path to stardom.

Burnett grew up in financial hardship in Los Angeles, raised primarily by her grandmother in a modest apartment, where dreams of performing seemed out of reach. While studying at UCLA and later performing at a junior-year student party in San Diego, she caught the attention of a businessman and his wife who made an intentional, extraordinary intervention: they offered Burnett and her fiancé Don Saroyan a $1,000 interest-free loan, sufficient at the time to move them to New York and pursue Broadway dreams.

The advocate made three specific conditions:

- Don't reveal his name
- Use the funds to move to New York
- And promise to help others if they find success

Burnett kept every promise, launching her stage career through nightclub gigs, the Rehearsal Club community, and eventually TV and Broadway roles. This timely, purposeful investment made possible her breakthrough, but her momentum was further accelerated by Lucille Ball, who became Burnett's mentor and champion in television, regularly advocating for her with producers, sharing advice and screen time, and staying a close friend for decades.

Burnett would later describe her success as a chain of "wonderful coincidences and intentional interventions", an unseen hand paying it forward in her life. Her career was a testament to the power of advocacy, mentorship, and a lasting legacy of helping others find their stage.

> The most powerful influence you'll have in Legacy-Level Living may be doors you open for people who can't open them themselves, or who don't yet realize what you've done.

You may never know the full impact, but that's not the point. Make the introduction. Open the door.

> God knows what He's about to do.

The Power of Strategic Open-Handed Advocacy

Advocacy is influence in action—using your voice, credibility, and relational capital on behalf of those who don't yet have access.

At this stage of life and leadership, you hold a kind of currency others can't yet earn. Your networks, your reputation, your accumulated credibility—all are forms of capital. The question isn't whether you have them. The question is whether you'll hoard them protectively or deploy them generously.

You now carry three forms of capital that define your Legacy-Level Living advantage:

Relational capital: the network you've built over decades.

Reputational capital: credibility earned through years of integrity and results.

Resource capital: access to opportunities, information, and platforms out of reach for others.

Strategic advocacy means intentionally spending that capital to create pathways for others. When you do, three things happen:

You remove barriers. You demonstrate belief in someone's potential. And you multiply more impact through them than you could ever produce alone.

This is the kind of power that humbles you as it expands you—the realization that your influence can now open doors others can't yet touch.

Turn today's 1440 minutes into momentum.
Download your free tracker at 1440Tracker.com

Three Forms of Strategic Advocacy

Introductions That Create Opportunity

You know Person A who should really meet Person B.
You send one short message:
"Person B, meet Person A. Here's why you should know each other."

That thirty-second gesture can alter someone's life trajectory. Your network becomes someone else's bridge.

You're positioned to see connections they can't. Introductions are tiny hinges that swing massive doors. Be known as the person who opens them.

Recommendations That Open Doors

A recommendation or reference transfers your reputation temporarily to someone else. When you vouch for them, your credibility covers them long enough for theirs to grow.

That's not small. That's legacy.
You remember who did that for you.

When you spend your credibility generously—without recklessness, but with faith—you extend your name as a covering umbrella that lets new voices step into rain they were unprepared for.

Advocacy in Rooms They're Not In

The hardest form, and the most Christlike, is advocacy for someone who cannot hear you doing it.

You're in a meeting, making a decision, having a conversation that could change someone's opportunity. You speak their name with confidence: "She's ready for this role." "He should be considered for that project."

They may never know what it cost you or realize how it changed them. But this invisible advocacy often becomes the turning point of another person's story.

You once benefited from such hidden mentoring.
Now it's your turn to practice it. This is how legacies reproduce!

Connecting It All

Recognition began your journey. You saw the hidden influences that shaped you. Transformation followed: gratitude turned awareness into renewed energy, which you redirected toward generosity.

Now the expression becomes visible.
Opening doors is gratitude becoming action.
It's saying through your deeds, "Doors were opened for me, and I open doors for others."

> This final turn completes the movement: from influenced to influencer, from recipient to resource. You now steward your influence as your sacred responsibility.

Jesus' Commissioning Pattern

The Great Commission (Matthew 28:18–20) wasn't just an instruction to preach, it was the pattern of replication.

Jesus modeled door-opening leadership. He called people, developed them, gave them authority, and then sent them to do the same.

"As the Father has sent me, I am sending you," He said (John 20:21). His goal wasn't dependence, it was deployment. He didn't build fans; He released apprentices.

Turn today's 1440 minutes into momentum.
Download your free tracker at 1440Tracker.com

Pastor and author, Bill Hull, In his series, Jesus Christ, Disciple Maker, The Disciple Making Pastor and The Disciple Making Church, summarizes Jesus' developmental pattern this way:

> **Tell them what's important.**
>
> **Tell them why it's important.**
>
> **Show them how.**
>
> **Do it with them.**
>
> **Let them do it, providing feedback.**
>
> **When they're ready, deploy them.**

That's what strategic advocacy looks like—building capacity, then stepping back so others can lead.

(Bill Hull is the one who identified that I had one more gift in that lunchtime conversation I told about back in the introduction.)

The Acts 1:8 sequence says, "You will be my witnesses in Jerusalem, Judea, Samaria, and to the ends of the earth." That's influence expanding in widening circles—near, extended, different, generational.

Every open door you create ripples through those circles:

> Jerusalem—family, team, close circle.
>
> Judea—professional network, extended relationships.
>
> Samaria—people outside your usual boundaries.
>
> Ends of the earth—those you'll never meet but will be reached through those you influence.

You will never see every effect, but that's the beauty. You're part of divine multiplication, not managing results but releasing them.

> Turn today's 1440 minutes into momentum.
> Download your free tracker at 1440Tracker.com

Making Door-Opening Practical

Inspiration without practice becomes sentiment.
Legacy requires rhythm. Start with three simple habits.

The Weekly Question:
Each week, ask, "Who needs a door opened?"
Check your calendar and network. It might take one short conversation, one introduction, one email. Over a year, that's fifty opportunities opened. Over a career, hundreds.

The Mentor's Mindset:
Ask, "Am I preparing someone for advancement or just improvement?"
Improvement keeps them better where they are. Advancement positions them for what's next. Legacy-minded mentoring prepares people for roles they can't yet imagine.

Advocate Courage:
"Who needs me to speak up?"
Advocacy occasionally costs political capital. That's okay—you have it to spend. Use your reliability to champion overlooked talent, underrepresented voices, or new ideas that deserve hearing.

Follow through after opening the door. Check on them. Stay engaged. It proves your investment wasn't symbolic—it was real.

What This Costs You

It costs time. Emotional bandwidth. Some political risk.
The energy it takes to care deeply. But what you gain outweighs every cost.

> Watching someone flourish because you used your influence on their behalf is one of leadership's purest joys.

You'll see loyalty deepen, vision expand, and your impact multiply through others. That's not theory, it's the measured return of invested influence.

Living Open-Handed

Legacy-level leaders live open-handed. They hold opportunity loosely and share generously. The clenched-fist approach (protecting platform, guarding advantage) feels safe but actually shrinks impact.

Open-handed living flows from abundance: believing there's enough to go around, that others' success doesn't diminish yours.

Here's what it looks like in practice:

> When opportunity better fits someone else, hand it to them.

> When you can recommend one person, recommend three.

When you're on a platform, highlight someone else's work.

When celebrating success, name your team before yourself.

When asked for help, give more than requested.

Open-handedness peaks in the succession mindset. Most try to be indispensable.

> We Legacy leaders aim to be unnecessary. We measure success by how well we prepared others to carry on.

That shift feels risky. We sometimes worry someone will surpass us. Let them. Their success expands your legacy.

Not every investment will flourish. Some doors you open won't lead where you hoped. But that's not failure. Influence that lives by faith invests knowing that results may remain unseen.

The freedom you have now allows this. You've proven yourself, built credibility, and earned security. You can stop guarding your place and start building theirs.

That— is fulfilling success! An advancer, more than an achiever. A blesser more than a builder. An influencer more than a success!

The Greater Reward

You began this journey identifying the people who influenced you. You learned gratitude, shifted metrics from arrival to legacy, integrated faith with your leadership, and discovered the joy of giving from what you've been given.

Now the reward emerges not in applause but in awareness. You're living your purpose.

The reward isn't comfort; it's contribution.
It isn't recognition, it's realization.
You're part of God's ongoing work of renewal in people and generations.

Fulfillment was never meant to be found at arrival. It's found in alignment with God's design, with others' flourishing, with a life spent on what will last.

When we live open-handed, we're finally free.
Did you notice? I said "we". That's on purpose. I hope you've decided "That's how I want to live!" We awaken each day knowing & remembering our purpose. It's a sacred purpose, yet it feels natural. We see potential in others because we've learned to see ourselves as stewards, not owners.

That's the greater reward—the true fulfillment of a life influencing the world as God intended. Not striving. Not proving. Simply living poured out, grateful, generous, and glad.

Our stories —your story— becomes part of theirs.
And through them, God keeps writing His.

Turn today's 1440 minutes into momentum.
Download your free tracker at 1440Tracker.com

Case Stories

Reba McEntire and the National Finals Rodeo National Anthem

Reba McEntire's ascent in country music was powered by intentional introductions and active advocacy at key moments. Born into a musical family on an Oklahoma ranch, Reba first gained local attention performing with her siblings as The Singing McEntires, before enrolling at Southeastern Oklahoma State University, intending to teach. The turning point came at the 1974 National Finals Rodeo, where her father and family friend Clem McSpadden helped her secure a gig singing the national anthem—a performance that drew the attention of country star Red Steagall.

Impressed by her acapella version of Dolly Parton's "Joshua" at a hotel party, Steagall invited Reba to record a demo tape and personally shopped it around Nashville, making formal introductions and leveraging his industry reputation to open doors, even when local labels were unsure about signing an untested female soloist. Ultimately, Glenn Keener at PolyGram/Mercury Records chose Reba's demo and offered her a contract—an intentional act of faith and mentorship that solidified her entry into mainstream country.

Reba's gate was not just opened by luck, but by heartfelt advocacy from Steagall, her mother Jacqueline's encouragement, and industry connections forged by her family. Their active championing transformed Reba's local talent into national opportunity, setting her up for a career defined by authenticity, resilience, and gratitude for those who lifted her over the threshold.

Turn today's 1440 minutes into momentum.
Download your free tracker at 1440Tracker.com

This space is reserved for notes about YOUR case stories!

Turn today's 1440 minutes into momentum.
Download your free tracker at 1440Tracker.com

LAB: Opening Doors Intentionally

Thinking Shift

From: "My job is to succeed and help when asked."

To: "It's my privilege to strategically open doors for people who can't open them for themselves."

Key Insight: At this stage, you have three forms of capital
- relational,
- reputational, and
- resource

that others don't yet have.
Strategic advocacy is a powerful form of multiplication: using your capital to unlock others' potential.

ACTION: The Strategic Advocacy Plan

Step 1: Capital Inventory (20 minutes)

Honestly assess what you have to leverage:

Relational Capital:

• Who do you know that others need access to?

• What networks, organizations, groups can you introduce people into?

• What relationships took you decades to build that you could share?

_____
_____
_____

Reputational Capital:

• Where does your recommendation carry weight?

• What opportunities can you advocate for others to receive?

• In what rooms can you speak credibly on someone's behalf?

_____
_____
_____

Resource Capital:

• What access do you have that others don't?
(information, tools, platforms)

• What opportunities can you create or share?

• What financial, material, or institutional resources can you deploy?

_____
_____
_____

Step 2: Identify Your Advocacy Targets (30 minutes)

The Overlooked: Who has potential others are missing?

• List 3 people with talent, character, or calling that's not being recognized

• Why are they being overlooked?
What do you see that others don't?

_____
_____
_____

The Blocked: Who has potential but lacks access?

• List 3 people with ability but no pathway forward

• What specific door would change their trajectory?

_____
_____
_____

The Ready: Who is prepared for the next level?

• List 3 people who are ready to advance but need an advocate

• What exactly do they need? Introduction? Recommendation? Opportunity?

_____
_____
_____

From these 9, choose 3 to focus on this quarter
(one from each category).

Step 3: Three Strategic Advocacy Actions (This quarter)

For each of your three targets, commit to ONE specific action:

Action Type Options:

❏ Introduction: Connect them with someone who can help them

❏ Recommendation: Write/speak on their behalf for opportunity

❏ Advocacy: Speak up for them in a room they're not in

❏ Platform Share: Give them access to your audience/network

❏ Resource Deploy: Use your capital to create opportunities they couldn't access alone

Implementation Plan:

• What exactly will you do?

_____
_____
_____

• When will you do it? (Put it on calendar)

_____
_____
_____

• What might it cost you? (time, political capital, reputation risk)

_____
_____
_____

• What preparation do they need? (Have the conversation first)

_____
_____
_____

- Note to self: How will I follow through?

_____

_____

Step 4: The Weekly Advocacy Question (Ongoing practice)

Add to weekly routine:
"Who needs a door opened this week?"

Keep a running list of:
- Introductions made
- Recommendations written
- Advocacy provided
- Doors opened

Checkpoint Milestone:

❏ *I've completed a capital inventory, identified 9 advocacy targets, taken strategic action to open doors for at least 3 people this quarter, and established the weekly advocacy question as ongoing practice.*

Scriptural Footings

On Strategic Advocacy:

- Esther 4:14 – For such a time
- Proverbs 31:8-9 – Speak up for those who cannot
- Isaiah 1:17 – Defend the oppressed
- Acts 9:26-27 – Barnabas vouches for Saul
- Philemon 8-21 – Paul advocates for Onesimus

On Opening Doors:

- Colossians 4:3 – Door for the message
- Acts 14:27 – Opened door of faith
- 1 Corinthians 16:9 – Wide door opened
- 2 Corinthians 2:12 – Door opened

On Using Your Influence:

- Luke 16:9 – Use worldly wealth
- Matthew 5:14-16 – Let your light shine
- Genesis 12:2 – Blessed to be a blessing
- Galatians 6:10 – Do good to all
- Proverbs 3:27-28 – Don't withhold good

On Seeing & Championing Potential:

- Acts 11:22-26 – Barnabas, son of encouragement
- 1 Samuel 16:7 – The Lord looks at the heart
- John 1:43-51 – Jesus calls Philip & Nathanael
- Mark 10:46-52 – Jesus sees blind Bartimaeus
- Luke 19:1-10 – Zacchaeus encounters Jesus

Turn today's 1440 minutes into momentum.
Download your free tracker at 1440Tracker.com

On Generous Use of Capital:

- Luke 12:48 – Much given, much required
- 1 Timothy 6:17-19 – Generous and willing to share
- Acts 4:32-37 – No one claimed possessions
- 2 Corinthians 8:1-5 – Macedonian generosity
- Romans 12:13 – Practice hospitality

On Making Introductions & Connections:

- Acts 9:26-27 – Barnabas introduces Saul
- Romans 16:1-2 – Commend Phoebe
- Colossians 4:7-9 – Tychicus and Onesimus
- Philippians 2:19-30 – Timothy and Epaphroditus
- 3 John 1:5-8 – Support fellow workers

On Legacy Through Others:

- 2 Timothy 2:2 – Teach to teach
- Matthew 28:18-20 – Make disciples
- Acts 1:8 – Witnesses to the ends
- John 14:12 – Greater works
- Psalm 145:4 – Generation to generation

INFLUENCED! - Conclusion

A friend of mine who married his high-school sweetheart enjoyed telling about their first kiss. In their mid-teens, usually group-dating, they managed to get off by themselves for a minute and he took a chance. He kissed her politely. She closed her eyes, anticipating the next kiss she knew was coming. Only it didn't. Gingerly opening her eyes, she saw him right there... "What?" she asked, bracing for the worst.

"Isn't this where the strings are supposed to come in?" he grinned. She smiled. Then he *kissed* her!

Did you happen to notice as you read this book, that the music never came in to give you a clue something important was about to happen? No sweet strings, no drum and bass cadence to build the tension. No Aida trumpets from atop the palace wall.
There's a reason for that:

> The beginning of transformation doesn't announce itself with fanfare.

The decision to shift from arrival to legacy happens in an ordinary moment—over morning coffee, during a commute, in the middle of an unremarkable Tuesday.

Turn today's 1440 minutes into momentum.
Download your free tracker at 1440Tracker.com

No dramatic music, no witnesses, no external validation,
Just a quiet internal shift:
"I'm going to live differently from here forward".

If you're expecting a dramatic moment, pause a second and note the date, maybe the time. Because if you've been reading with openness, you've already started — the shift is underway!

Unlike arrival milestones (those DO come with fanfare: promotion announcements, awards ceremonies, public recognition),

Legacy-milestones are quiet:
  decision to mentor,
  choice to open a door,
  commitment to model character—no one applauds.

But these quiet decisions create ripples you'll never fully see.
Let this book's cover remind you of that truth.

You don't need anyone's permission or applause to begin; you just begin. And in a way, that's to your benefit. You can gain momentum quickly if you want. You can falter a couple of times and no one will notice.

> You've no one to impress,
> nothing to prove.

Turn today's 1440 minutes into momentum.
Download your free tracker at 1440Tracker.com

You're establishing a new norm, Legacy-Level Living, that's consistent with your character and demeanor.
No one has to notice — yet. Eventually they may. Some will take the time or make the effort to thank you.

Have your smile ready, and a softspoken "It was a pleasure," or something similar.

Then, silently and without fanfare (again), do what I taught my musicians to do for years. (I learned this from Derric Johnson, leader of The Re'Generation.) Imagine their compliment as a perfect rose. Smell its sweet fragrance, lift it up, and in silent worship give it to your Savior:

This— belongs to You.

Your Transformation Summary:

You began by recognizing the people who have influenced your life including hidden mentors whose contributions helped shape you, and actively expressed your gratitude.

As your perspective shifted from arrival-based achievement to legacy-building metrics, you've intentionally reallocated your time and energy toward what lasts.

You moved beyond gratitude as a feeling to gratitude fueling ongoing generous action, and established your rhythm of tangible generosity.

Integrating your faith with your daily work, you started measuring impact by the growth and capacity you fostered in others. These new forms of investment are becoming increasingly rewarding.

Turn today's 1440 minutes into momentum.
Download your free tracker at 1440Tracker.com

And you've stepped up, intentionally using your influence to open doors for others, advocating for people and weaving strategic generosity into your weekly habits. As a result, your fulfillment is deeper than it's ever been and you're amplifying your impact.

You began UNAWARE of how profoundly you've been influenced.

You end as a STRATEGIC ADVOCATE who:

- Recognizes lineage with gratitude
- Discovers invisible influence with humility
- Measures success by contribution, not accumulation
- Gives generously from renewed abundance
- Integrates faith with work through daily integrity
- Multiplies influence by opening doors strategically

This is Legacy-Level Living!

A Note from me in your desk drawer—

You've— been INFLUENCED!

Family members, mentors, hidden investors whose names you're still discovering, have all helped shape who you've become.

You're now poised to influence others, and the shift is pure delight.
You're stewarding. Not from obligation but from overflow.
Not from guilt but from gratitude.

The doors opened for you position you to open doors for others.

Your accumulated wisdom is currency for others' development.

The resources you've gathered are for circulation, not accumulation.

There was no fanfare — you just quietly, faithfully began, trusting small investments would compound over time into influence that outlasts you.

Go now —   Steward what you've been given.
           Open doors.
           Influence intentionally.

Your Legacy-Level Living is waiting.
Smile when people begin to say —maybe they already are—
"I've been INFLUENCED!" and they mean by you!

Phil

Turn today's 1440 minutes into momentum.
Download your free tracker at 1440Tracker.com

For Further Reading

While this is not a Bibliography, these books and authors will add worthy material for you to explore as you develop your approach to intentional investing in others.

Purpose, Calling, and Life Direction

· Bosché, Gabrielle, and Brian Bosché. *The Purpose Factor: Extreme Clarity for Why You're Here and What to Do About It.* Post Hill Press, ©2022. ISBN 9781637589199.

· Buford, Bob. *Halftime: Changing Your Game Plan from Success to Significance.* Zondervan, ©1994. ISBN 0310257794.

· Green, David, with Bill High. *The Legacy Life: How to Build Generations of Influence and Impact.* Baker Books, ©2025. ISBN 9781540904805.

· Swindoll, Charles R. *Living Above the Level of Mediocrity.* Word Publishing, ©1987. ISBN 0849905648.

Influence, Relationships, and Leadership

· Barrett, Morag. *Cultivate: The Power of Winning Relationships* (2nd ed.). River Grove Books, ©2025. ISBN 9781632999740.

· Freschi, Dan. *Where Leadership Begins.* Nico 11 Publishing & Design, ©2023. ISBN 9781957351247

· Morgan, Angie, and Courtney Lynch. *Bet on You: How to Win with Risk.* HarperCollins Leadership, ©2022. ISBN 9781400229796.

Turn today's 1440 minutes into momentum.
Download your free tracker at 1440Tracker.com

· Sun, Lisa, with Huck, Kathryn. *Gravitas: Communicate with Confidence, Influence and Authority.* Hay House, Inc, ©2023. ISBN 9781401972530.

Spiritual Formation and Discipleship

· Hull, Bill. *Jesus Christ, Disciplemaker* (20th anniversary ed.). Baker Books, ©2004. ISBN 9780801091698.

· McNeal, Reggie. *A Work of Heart: Understanding How God Shapes Spiritual Leaders.* Jossey-Bass, ©2000. ISBN 078794288X.

· Murphy, Jonathan. *The Authentic Influencer: The Barnabas Way of Shaping Lives for Jesus.* Thomas Nelson, ©2023. ISBN 9781400333301.

· Hendricks, Howard G. *The 7 Laws of the Teacher.* Walk Thru the Bible Ministries, ©1995. ISBN 0880701986.

Focus, Margin, and Sustainable Impact

· McKeown, Greg. *Essentialism: The Disciplined Pursuit of Less.* Crown Business (Currency), ©2014. ISBN 9780804137386.

· McKeown, Greg. *Effortless: Make It Easier to Do What Matters Most.* Currency (Crown Publishing Group), ©2021. ISBN 9780593135648.

· Sinek, Simon. *Start with Why: How Great Leaders Inspire Everyone to Take Action.* Portfolio, ©2009. ISBN 9781591842804.

Turn today's 1440 minutes into momentum.
Download your free tracker at 1440Tracker.com

Free Resource: Your 1440 Tracker

Before you close this book, let's turn your intention into action.

I've created a free tool called The 1440 Tracker.

It's a daily reminder to invest in people and opportunities.

The 1440 Tracker helps you steward your daily "1440-minute auto-deposit"

with purpose, gratitude, and strategic generosity. It's designed

to keep you focused on what truly matters: who you're

becoming and who's better because of you.

Download your free tracker at **www.1440Tracker.com**

and begin your legacy-level journey today.

Bring Phil to Your Event

If this book has challenged your thinking about influence and

legacy, imagine what happens when I bring these principles to your

stage! Instead of another "motivational talk", I bring transformation

frameworks that guide your audience to discover their purpose,

redefine success & fulfillment and heighten their long-range impact.

Turn today's 1440 minutes into momentum.
Download your free tracker at 1440Tracker.com

Here are three topics that consistently resonate with audiences:

1. Return on Invested Influence: The ROI² Framework

How to measure what truly matters and purposefully invest in others for

multiplied influence. ROI² outperforms the metrics on your current dashboard.

2. The Art of Thriving: 5 Secrets to True Success That aren't Secrets at All

Months —even years— of consistent effort precede every award-winning

performance, major accomplishment, or breakthrough. When purpose, vision, strategy,

—*and two more I'll tell you about*— converge long-term, celebrations result.

3. Strategic Advocacy: Opening Doors That Change Lives

The practical and rewarding framework for intentionally using your influence to benefit others.

Why opening doors and selflessly connecting people exponentially multiplies your impact.

If you'd like me to speak at your next event, conference, or

leadership gathering, let's connect.

Reach out at

Phil@PhilRansom.com.

Turn today's 1440 minutes into momentum.
Download your free tracker at 1440Tracker.com

Made in the USA
Coppell, TX
29 December 2025

67533042R00089